To My
MustangMan, John

On His
Big 9

Love,
DAD

SUPER CARS

SUPER CARS

GENERAL EDITOR: CRAIG CHEETHAM

MOTORBOOKS
INTERNATIONAL

This edition published in 2003 by Motorbooks International, an imprint of MBI Publishing Company, Galtier Plaza, Suite 200, 380 Jackson Street, St. Paul, MN 55101-3885 USA

Copyright © 2003 International Masters Publishers AB
Introduction text copyright © 2003 Amber Books Ltd

Motorbooks International titles are also available at discounts in bulk quantity for industrial or sales-promotional use. For details write to Special Sales Manager at Motorbooks International Wholesalers & Distributors, Galtier Plaza, Suite 200, 380 Jackson Street, St. Paul, MN 55101-3885 USA.

ISBN 0-7603-1685-6

Produced by:
Amber Books Ltd
Bradley's Close
74–77 White Lion Street
London N1 9PF
www.amberbooks.co.uk

Printed in Italy

All photographs © International Masters Publishers AB except 6,7 © EMAP Automotive

This material was previously published as part of the reference set *Hot Cars*

CONTENTS

Introduction

What exactly is a supercar? There is no definitive answer, yet the term is widely accepted by car enthusiasts to decribe an exotic, powerful and expensive car that represents the ultimate in performance, styling and pure, unadulterated driving thrills.

Yet a supercar can take one of many forms. It can be a strictly limited production special such as the McLaren F1, which features an engine bay lined with platinum and is capable of 230mph, and costs over a million dollars to buy. Or it can be a car like the Lancia Thema 8.32—externally it is little different from a standard saloon, but underneath the ordinary-looking hood lurks the heart of a beast, a massive Ferrari unit that develops as much power as the Italian style icons themselves.

A supercar is a very personal machine—one that appeals because it is the very best of its kind. Naturally, many supercars come from the elite of the world's carmakers. Names like Aston Martin, Ferrari, Lamborghini, Maserati, and Porsche need no introduction. Each of these names stands for power and beauty, and each

manufacturer is represented here by their finest machines—some of the most stunning cars the world has ever seen.

Motoring's more mainstream names are featured in this book too. Honda's NSX, for example, is one of the finest-handling cars on the planet, yet comes from the same manufacturer as the compact Civic and family-oriented Accord. With a top speed of 170mph on the range-topping NSX-R, nobody can deny it has earned its place among the elite. The same can be said of the Audi RS2. The subtle German station wagon has four-wheel-drive and an engine developed by Porsche, making it stunningly quick and deeply desirable.

Then there are the manufacturers on the fringe of the car industry, who specialize in building machines that appeal to hardcore enthusiasts rather than the masses. Britain's TVR, America's Ultima and France's Venturi all fit into this category and they all have one thing in

Produced to celebrate the company's 40th birthday, the Ferrari F40 was a barely-tamed racer for the road.

common: their cars are built with a passion and intricacy that none of the bigger players can match in their state-of-the-art factories.

This book also includes the cars built as specials in order to qualify the model for racing and rallying. The Ford RS200 is based on the humble Sierra, yet is a mindblowing performance machine that demands precision driving—only the bravest need apply. Then there is the Lancia 037 Rally. This mid-engined masterpiece was one of the ultimate Group B rally cars. It went like a rocket, but needed serious mastery behind the steering wheel to stop it flying off course. It recalls an era of motorsport that, because of safety legislation, will never be seen again.

And finally, this book also includes some of America's most potent performance icons. The tire-shredding V10 Dodge Viper, the legendary AC Superblower, the race-tuned Callaway Corvette Speedster, and the awesome Shelby CSX are all burning their rubber on these pages, and this book puts you so close to the action you can practically smell it.

When the creator of the Ferrari 250 GTO set out to build a competitor, the result was bound to be spectacular. The Bizzarrini GT Strada is a rare and beautiful beast.

Whatever your definition of a supercar, you're bound to find something in this book that fuels your desire. We've grouped together some of the world's most desirable machines in these pages. Millions of dollars, thousands of horsepower, and a combined top speed that would make space travel look slow will leave you awed. These are the cars that grace the driveways of millionaire playboys, yet to the mere mortal they're practically unobtainable. We hope you'll find this book the next best thing. We can't put you in the driving seat of these monstrous machines, but we can give you expert opinions from those lucky enough to have spent time behind the wheel.

So read our driving impressions and marvel at the performance figures, admire the flowing lines and brutal powerplants, then close your eyes and imagine yourself at the helm of one of these true thoroughbreds.

AC **SUPERBLOWER**

With the company in new hands, AC replaced the 225-bhp Cobra Mk IV with a new model. The earth-shattering Superblower uses a supercharger to redress the power loss through emissions equipment.

"...a real retro racer."

"If it weren't for the stylish new dashboard and modern gauges, you would think you were sitting in a 1965 Cobra. A further clue to the car's age is given when you start the engine. There's the telltale whine of a supercharger from under the hood. Floor the throttle and hang on. This retro racer will give you a ride that is second to none. On a twisty road, a modern hot sedan would probably cover ground faster, but nothing can beat the AC in a straight line."

The Superblower's dashboard is much neater than that in its predecessor, the Cobra Mk IV.

Milestones

1962 Texan Carroll Shelby creates the AC Cobra—an AC Ace with a Ford V8 squeezed under the hood.

1985 The Cobra is reborn as the Cobra Mk IV after 17 years out of production.

The original Cobra first hit the street way back in 1962.

1996 Pride Automotive takes over AC Cars and the rights to build the Cobra.

The Superblower uses the wide-arched body of the Mk III Cobra.

1997 The newly named AC Car Group shows the AC Superblower. A new Cobra variant, it uses a supercharged 5.0-liter Ford V8 producing 355 bhp. It redresses the performance loss suffered by the Cobra Mk IV, which ended its life with only 225 bhp.

UNDER THE SKIN

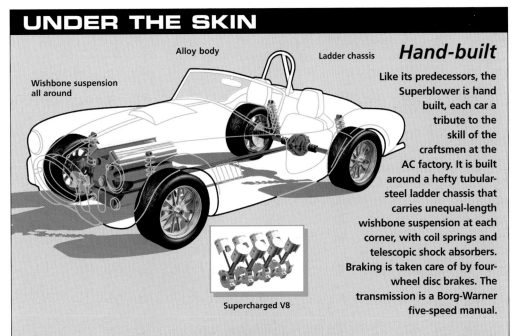

Wishbone suspension all around

Alloy body

Ladder chassis

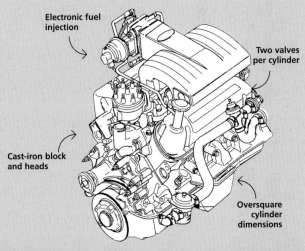

Supercharged V8

Hand-built

Like its predecessors, the Superblower is hand built, each car a tribute to the skill of the craftsmen at the AC factory. It is built around a hefty tubular-steel ladder chassis that carries unequal-length wishbone suspension at each corner, with coil springs and telescopic shock absorbers. Braking is taken care of by four-wheel disc brakes. The transmission is a Borg-Warner five-speed manual.

THE POWER PACK

Bad and blown

The Superblower uses the same 5.0-liter V8 in the pre-1996 Ford Mustang GT. The engine, which arrives in a crate from the U.S., has been modified by the Ford Special Vehicle Team to better accommodate the supercharger fitted by AC at the factory. Whereas this engine, used in naturally aspirated form, produced only 225 bhp and 300 lb-ft in the Cobra Mk IV, it now cranks out a huge 355 bhp at 5,700 rpm in the Superblower and an even more impressive 385 lb-ft at 3,750 rpm.

Electronic fuel injection

Two valves per cylinder

Cast-iron block and heads

Oversquare cylinder dimensions

Super snake

The Superblower is a much better development of the original Cobra theme than the Mk IV. Its supercharged engine gives the car the kind of terrifying tire-frying acceleration that made the original so famous back in the 1960s. Its look is as deadly as its bite.

With 355 bhp, the Superblower is a Cobra-derivative with some real bite.

AC **SUPERBLOWER**

It may look like the Cobra of the 1960s, but the new AC Superblower adds a supercharger for extra performance thrills. Off the line, there is still little to beat this muscular V8-engined AC sports car.

Supercharged V8

The Superblower uses the 5.0-liter Ford V8 commonly found in the pre-1996 Mustang GT. In this case, the engine has been breathed on by Ford Special Vehicle Operations and fitted with a supercharger to take maximum power up to 355 bhp. It's enough to take the AC to its limited top speed of 155 mph.

Ladder chassis

Like its forebears, the Superblower uses a separate ladder chassis with the two main longitudinal members in large-diameter steel tube, and smaller-diameter tubing used for the crossmembers.

Chrome roll bar

The driver's chrome roll bar is standard on the Superblower. It resembles that used on competition Cobras in the 1960s and protects the driver if the car rolls.

Wishbone suspension

Suspension is by unequal-length wishbones front and rear. Coil springs and telescopic shock absorbers are used all around.

Luxury interior

The interior is traditionally hand-crafted using top-quality leather and deep-pile wool carpeting. The old Cobra Mk IV dashboard was redesigned for the Superblower.

1960s-style wheels

The knock-on alloy wheels resemble the styling of the Halibrand racing wheels often fitted to the 1965 Mk III Cobra.

Hand-crafted bodywork

The Superblower's body is constructed from 16-gauge aluminum alloy, hand-rolled by AC craftsmen and seam-welded for a tidy finish.

Specifications

1998 AC Superblower

ENGINE

Type: V8

Construction: Cast-iron block and heads

Valve gear: Two valves per cylinder operated by a single camshaft via pushrods and rockers

Bore and stroke: 4.0 in. x 3.0 in.

Displacement: 5.0 liter

Compression ratio: 9.0:1

Induction system: Sequential electronic fuel injection with a centrifugal supercharger

Maximum power: 355 bhp at 5,700 rpm

Maximum torque: 385 lb-ft at 3,750 rpm

TRANSMISSION

Five-speed manual

BODY/CHASSIS

Steel ladder chassis with aluminum two-door open sports car body

SPECIAL FEATURES

A racing-style fuel filler cap sets off the Superblower's 1960s styling.

A supercharger takes the power of the 5.0-liter Ford V8 to 355 bhp.

RUNNING GEAR

Steering: Rack-and-pinion

Front suspension: Double wishbones with coil springs and telescopic shock absorbers

Rear suspension: Double wishbones with coil springs and telescopic shock absorbers

Brakes: Discs (front and rear)

Wheels: Alloy, 16-in. dia.

Tires: 225/50 VR16 (front), 255/50 VR16 (rear)

DIMENSIONS

Length: 165.4 in.   **Width:** 68.7 in.

Height: 47.2 in.   **Wheelbase:** 90.0 in.

Track: 55.5 in. (front), 58.5 in. (rear)

Weight: 2,558 lbs.

Alpine **A610**

With performance and handling to rival the Porsche 911, the rear-engined Alpine A610 should have been a success. But Alpine learned that people won't pay for a supercar that doesn't have the right name and badge.

"...no shortage of power."

"Despite the engine being hung out at the back beyond the transmission and the rear axle line, the Alpine will not bite; lift off the accelerator in corners and the tail will swing out wide. The A610 has masses of grip, immediate turn-in to corners, and very responsive handling. There's no shortage of power and the turbo installation is geared for strong mid-range torque, so there is virtually no lag. The car's only real weakness is its slight 'kit-car' appearance."

Luxury is leather-clad inside the A610. The driving position is comfortable for all but the tallest drivers.

Milestones

1955 Société Automobiles Alpine

is formed by Jean Redélé to build sporting Renault-engined cars, starting with the A106.

The four-cylinder A110 was a successful rally car.

1963 A110s are built

with different engines and power outputs. Renault takes over Alpine the following year.

The A310 is the first to receive the Renault V6 engine.

1971 A310 appears

with a Renault 16TX engine before being given a V6.

1984 A610's direct

ancestor, the V6GT, is launched in naturally aspirated and turbo form.

1990 Le Mans

limited edition of the V6GT is launched; it is more powerful and faster.

1991 Visitors to the

Geneva Motor Show get the first look at the new A610 with its pop-up lights, revised chassis and running gear.

UNDER THE SKIN

Steel backbone

All Alpines have had fiberglass bodies and rear-mounted engines. A610s have a central steel backbone with pressed-steel sections holding the double wishbone and coil spring front suspension. Double wishbones are used at the rear too, held along with the engine in a detachable subframe, so the whole rear end can be removed for overhaul. The fiberglass body is bonded to the chassis, increasing strength.

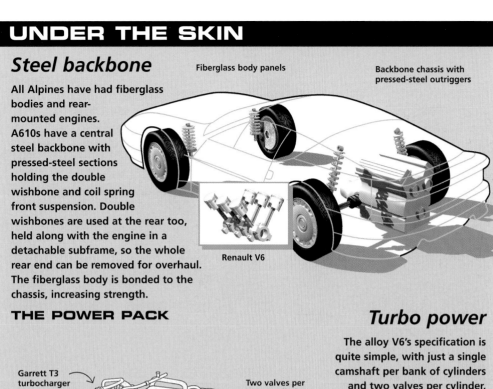

Fiberglass body panels

Backbone chassis with pressed-steel outriggers

Renault V6

THE POWER PACK

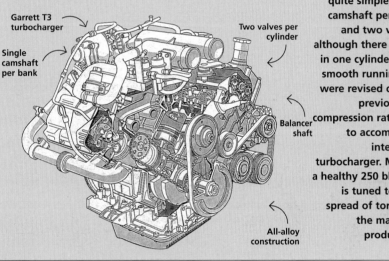

Garrett T3 turbocharger

Single camshaft per bank

Two valves per cylinder

Balancer shaft

All-alloy construction

Turbo power

The alloy V6's specification is quite simple, with just a single camshaft per bank of cylinders and two valves per cylinder, although there is a balancer shaft in one cylinder bank to promote smooth running. Cylinder heads were revised compared with the previous Alpine, and the compression ratio was a low 7.6:1 to accommodate the single intercooled Garrett T3 turbocharger. Maximum power is a healthy 250 bhp, but the engine is tuned to give a very wide spread of torque, 95 percent of the maximum 258 lb-ft is produced from 2,000 to 5,200 rpm.

Flawed but fun

The predecessor to the A610, the V6GT has less performance ability than the A610 and trickier handling, but its styling is purer and it requires more from the driver to get the best out of the car. The A610 is almost too easy to drive.

The GTA was less refined, but a more rewarding driver's car.

Alpine **A610**

The first of the long Alpine line which could really aspire to join the supercar league, the stylish A610 uses a Garrett turbocharger to extract 250 bhp from its rear-mounted V6 engine.

Low drag coefficient

The A610 really is as sleek as it looks, with a drag coefficient of just 0.30. That helps both outright speed and fuel economy, which is excellent for a 150-mph-plus car.

Intercooled turbocharger

Although the V6 uses only a single turbocharger instead of one for each bank of cylinders, it has an air-to-air intercooler which increases power output.

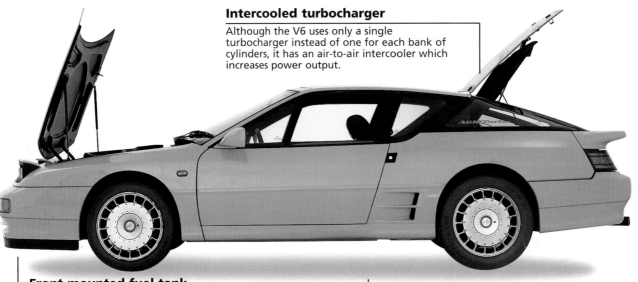

Front-mounted fuel tank

With rear-engined cars the designers move whatever they can to the front to help overall weight distribution. In this case the fuel tank is in the front, along with the spacesaver spare tire. Unfortunately, there's no front luggage space.

Pressed-steel backbone chassis

All Alpines have separate steel chassis: the A610's is a pressed-steel design with a welded-on steel floorpan which is bonded to the fiberglass bodywork.

Rear weight distribution

Weight distribution was improved for the A610 so that 57 percent of the weight is at the rear, making the car far less tricky to drive.

Large rear tires

With the engine at the back the majority of the weight is over the rear wheels. The rear Michelin 245/45 ZR16 tires are significantly larger than those fitted at the front.

Pop-up headlights

One contentious thing about the A610's revised styling, compared with the previous V6GT, was the switch to pop-up lights in place of large glass covers.

V6 engine

The A610's 3-liter engine is a modified Renault all-alloy V6 with fuel injection and a single chain-driven overhead cam per bank of cylinders.

Specifications

1992 Alpine A610

ENGINE

Type: V6
Construction: Alloy block and heads
Valve gear: Two inclined valves per cylinder operated by single chain-driven overhead cam per bank of cylinders via rockers
Bore and stroke: 3.66 in. x 2.87 in.
Displacement: 2,975 cc
Compression ratio: 7.6:1
Induction system: Electronic fuel injection with Garrett T3 turbocharger and intercooler
Maximum power: 250 bhp at 5,750 rpm
Maximum torque: 258 lb-ft at 2,900 rpm

TRANSMISSION

Five-speed manual

BODY/CHASSIS

Steel backbone chassis with rear subframe and bonded-on fiberglass hatchback coupe body

SPECIAL FEATURES

Side vents were added in front of the rear wheels to channel cooling air to the rear brakes and engine compartment.

The large windshield wipers don't move in a hand clapping motion, but in a complicated pattern designed to clear the maximum area of glass.

RUNNING GEAR

Steering: Rack-and-pinion
Front suspension: Double wishbones with coil springs, telescopic shocks and anti-roll bar
Rear suspension: Double wishbones with coil springs, telescopic shocks and anti-roll bar
Brakes: Vented discs, 11.8 in. dia. (front and rear)
Wheels: Alloy 7 in. x 16 in. (front), 9 in. x 16 in. (rear)
Tires: Michelin MXX 205/45 ZR16 (front), 245/45 ZR16 (rear)

DIMENSIONS

Length: 173.8 in.   **Width:** 69.4 in.
Wheelbase: 92.1 in.   **Height:** 46.8 in.
Track: 59.2 in. (front), 57.9 in. (rear)
Weight: 3,043 lbs.

Aston Martin **VIRAGE**

When it was introduced in 1988, the Virage was the first new Aston Martin model in 20 years. The result was a 330-bhp luxury heavyweight that was high on style.

"...a big, heavyweight cruiser."

"If you want real out-of-this-world performance you buy the 550-bhp Vantage version. The Virage is for those who want style, exclusivity and luxury with more performance than most cars in its class. It isn't a small, responsive sports car, so it will roll noticeably around tight corners, and requires the heavy ZF transmission quickly. The Virage will put up with the abuse, but it's more of a big, heavyweight cruiser, in its element on fast open roads."

While not in the Lamborghini Diablo league, Virage performance is still magnificent.

Milestones

1986 New Aston starts life as project DP2034; the brief is to build a car suitable for all world markets, one which can stay in production for many years.

The old Aston Martin V8 was long overdue for replacement.

1988 Styled by John Heffernan and Ken Greenley, the Virage makes its debut at the Birmingham Motor Show, going on sale the following year.

1990 Convertible Volante model is introduced.

Volante combined high performance with top-down appeal.

1992 Sporty estate version—the Shooting Brake is launched, followed by a tuned version of the Virage with an extra 135 bhp.

1993 Aston adds a supercharger to the 5.3 liter to make the 186-mph Vantage.

1996 Virage is updated with softer lines and 350 bhp.

UNDER THE SKIN

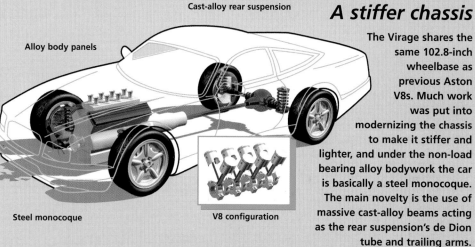

Cast-alloy rear suspension

Alloy body panels

Steel monocoque

V8 configuration

A stiffer chassis

The Virage shares the same 102.8-inch wheelbase as previous Aston V8s. Much work was put into modernizing the chassis to make it stiffer and lighter, and under the non-load bearing alloy bodywork the car is basically a steel monocoque. The main novelty is the use of massive cast-alloy beams acting as the rear suspension's de Dion tube and trailing arms.

THE POWER PACK

Better breathing

Corvette tuner Reeves Callaway helped revise the alloy V8's cylinder heads with a narrower valve angle which improved airflow, and also relocated the camshafts so they are closer together. These extensive modifications helped produce a more flexible engine with better throttle response in addition to increasing the engine's power. Output went up by only 21 bhp compared with the previous 32-valve unit. The engine is hand built by Aston craftsmen.

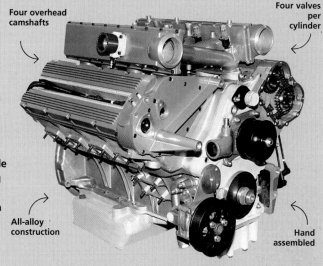

Four overhead camshafts

Four valves per cylinder

All-alloy construction

Hand assembled

Twin-charger

If you're hungry for power and don't mind spending some extra money you could order the staggeringly powerful Vantage version. The 5.3-liter V8 is given twin superchargers to boost power to 550 bhp, and top speed to 186 mph.

Wider arches, low spoilers and front fender louvers say 'Vantage.'

Aston Martin VIRAGE 🇬🇧

Its sleek lines cannot hide the sheer size or the brutal look of the Virage. It radiates power and performance but with leather-trimmed exclusivity.

High-profile tires

Early Virages ride on 60-profile tires where other supercars use lower-profile tires. The later, more powerful Vantage version uses even lower-profile tires.

Hand-built engine

Each Aston Martin V8 is assembled by one man. There's a plaque on each engine to show who assembled it.

Twin fuel fillers

The thirsty Virage has two fuel fillers to feed its large tank. The fillers are located on the top of the quarter panels near the rear quarter glass.

Steel skeleton

The Virage is not quite a true monocoque, where the whole bodyshell is part of the structure, as none of the external panels are load bearing.

Alloy body panels

In Aston tradition, the body panels are all aluminum-alloy and finished by hand. Even with those alloy panels, an alloy engine and alloy suspension components, the Aston is still a true heavyweight at 3,940 lbs.

Outboard rear brakes

Often with a de Dion system, the rear brakes can be mounted inboard. Aston kept them in the conventional place next to the wheel for improved cooling.

ZF five-speed transmission

To withstand the massive torque produced, Aston Martin chose a tough German ZF unit. In the tuned Vantage version, a six-speed is used.

Audi and VW lights

Even though Aston Martin makes its own engines, chassis and bodies, some parts are still bought in. The headlights come from the Audi 100 while the rear lights are borrowed from VW.

Front-biased weight distribution

Though the fierce V8 is alloy and mounted well back in the engine bay, the Virage is still nose heavy with a 54/46 front-to-rear weight distribution.

Specifications
1991 Aston Martin Virage

ENGINE

Type: V8

Construction: Alloy block and heads with wet liners

Valve gear: Four valves per cylinder operated by four overhead chain-driven cams

Bore and stroke: 3.93 in. x 3.34 in.

Displacement: 5,340 cc

Compression ratio: 9.5:1

Induction system: Weber-Marelli electronic fuel injection

Maximum power: 330 bhp at 6,000 rpm

Maximum torque: 340 lb-ft at 3,700 rpm

TRANSMISSION

ZF five-speed manual

BODY/CHASSIS

Steel semi-monocoque with alloy body panels and two-door, 2+2 coupe body

SPECIAL FEATURES

Virage rear seating for two is comfortable, but not very spacious.

It uses a space-saver for a spare wheel.

RUNNING GEAR

Steering: Rack-and-pinion

Front suspension: Double wishbones with coil springs, shocks and anti-roll bar

Rear suspension: De Dion axle with trailing arms, Watt linkage, coil springs and telescopic shocks

Brakes: Discs, vented 13 in. dia. (front), solid 11.1 in. dia. (rear)

Wheels: Alloy 8 in. x 16 in.

Tires: Avon Turbospeed 225/60 ZR16

DIMENSIONS

Length: 188 in.

Width: 72.8 in.

Height: 52.3 in.

Wheelbase: 102.8 in.

Track: 55 in. (front), 56.3 in. (rear)

Weight: 3,940 lbs.

Aston Martin ZAGATO

When Aston Martin wanted a car to make an instant impact and revitalize its ageing models it turned to Zagato—the master stylists from Milan. The brief was to build a supercar capable of reaching over 180 mph, that had dramatic looks and handling to match.

"...a genuine 180 mph."

"Cruise at 100 mph, floor the throttle and the performance envelope opens up. Beyond 3,000 rpm the Zagato comes into its own, hurling the heavyweight to a genuine 180 mph. The Zagato is quick off the line too, reaching 60 mph in less than 5 seconds. Yet, despite this, it's very easy to drive, with fine visibility and superb seats. The chassis is set up for mild understeer, but the independent suspension keeps the tires firmly planted at all times."

Even inside, the Zagato has very distinctive sharp-edge styling.

Milestones

1984 Aston Martin Chairman

Victor Gauntlett meets Gianni Zagato at the Geneva Motor Show and discusses plans for a car that will lift Aston's image and remind the world about Zagato design. Styling sketches are soon produced and orders worth almost $7 million are taken by Aston Martin just on the car's appearance.

A small number of Aston Martin GTs were bodied by Zagato.

1986 The Zagato goes into

limited production with the intention of building just 50 coupes. The rolling chassis are sent to Zagato's Milan factory for body and trim.

The handsome Virage replaced the Zagato in 1989.

1987 Aston Martin displays

the Zagato Volante convertible at the Geneva Show.

1989 Production stops,

with 50 coupes and 25 convertibles built.

UNDER THE SKIN

Nothing new

Although outwardly different, the Zagato has a V8 Vantage floorpan, shortened by 16 inches. It also uses the V8s double wishbone front suspension coupled to a de Dion rear end which allows the huge rear vented discs to be mounted inboard next to the final drive. The transmission, however, is mounted behind the engine, rather than at the rear axle, resulting in a noticeably front-heavy weight distribution.

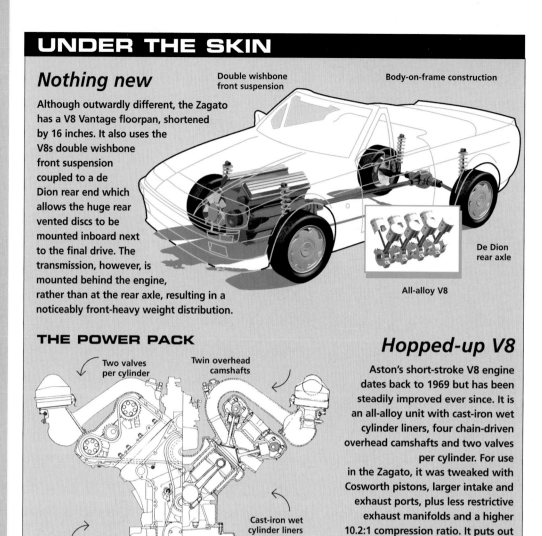

Double wishbone front suspension

Body-on-frame construction

De Dion rear axle

All-alloy V8

THE POWER PACK

Two valves per cylinder

Twin overhead camshafts

Cast-iron wet cylinder liners

Alloy block and cylinder heads

Hopped-up V8

Aston's short-stroke V8 engine dates back to 1969 but has been steadily improved ever since. It is an all-alloy unit with cast-iron wet cylinder liners, four chain-driven overhead camshafts and two valves per cylinder. For use in the Zagato, it was tweaked with Cosworth pistons, larger intake and exhaust ports, plus less restrictive exhaust manifolds and a higher 10.2:1 compression ratio. It puts out a mighty 432 bhp. The engine relies on four Weber carburetors for feeding the fuel.

Going topless

The Zagato Volante is even rarer than the coupe, and at the time of its introduction was the fastest convertible on the road. Launched in 1987, only 25 had been built by the time production ceased in 1989. Not surprisingly, they are highly sought after.

Aston Martin made twice as many Zagato coupes as it did Volante convertibles.

Aston Martin ZAGATO 🇬🇧

Zagato had the reputation of styling cars unlike any other. Here it went for a short car with tall wheels and a blunt aggressive look which radiated power, performance and exclusivity.

V8 engine

At the time the Zagato had the most powerful version of the aluminum Aston Martin quad-cam V8 engine. Revisions to the camshaft, cylinder head ports and carburetors helped to increase power to 432 bhp from its 5.3 liters. This output was more impressive than the peak torque as the engine was tuned for outright power.

ZF transmission

Aston used the tough German ZF five-speed manual transmission. It featured a dog leg first gear with the rest of the gears in the normal 'H' pattern.

De Dion axle

De Dion axles were popular with Aston Martin. They served the purpose of keeping the rear wheels upright at all times with none of the camber changes.

Short rear overhang

Zagato made its design look more compact than the existing Vantage by chopping 12 inches from the rear, reducing the size of the trunk. Extra luggage could be placed behind the front seats.

Lancia seats

With Zagato in charge of all interior trim, it chose Lancia Delta S4 front seats. These were trimmed in top-quality leather like all Aston Martin seats.

Foam bumpers

One way in which Zagato lightened the Aston was by discarding the steel bumpers and designing deformable foam-filled replacements mounted on hydraulic rams.

In-board discs

In theory, with a de Dion axle the logical place to mount the brakes is inboard next to the final drive, and that's where Aston put them.

Alloy body

Zagato was the master craftsmen in aluminum bodywork and made all the panels for the car, mounted on a modified form of the existing folded and welded sheet-metal substructure. All the panels were formed over a full-size wooden template.

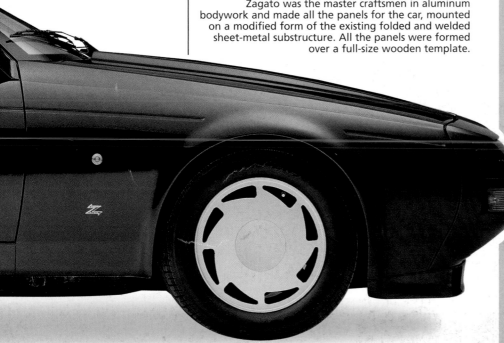

Specifications

1987 Aston Martin Zagato

ENGINE

Type: V8

Construction: Alloy block and heads

Valve gear: Two valves per cylinder operated by four chain-driven overhead camshafts

Bore and stroke: 3.93 in. x 3.35 in.

Displacement: 5,340 cc

Compression ratio: 10.2:1

Induction system: Four downdraft Weber IDF carburetors

Maximum power: 432 bhp at 6,200 rpm

Maximum torque: 395 lb-ft at 5,100 rpm

TRANSMISSION

TorqueFlite 727 five-speed automatic

BODY/CHASSIS

Steel substructure with alloy two-door coupe body

SPECIAL FEATURES

Volantes are distinguished from Zagato coupes by their headlight covers.

With its shortened tail and convertible top, the Volante's trunk space is limited.

RUNNING GEAR

Steering: Rack-and-pinion

Front suspension: Double wishbones with coil springs, Koni shock absorbers and anti-roll bar

Rear suspension: Rigid de Dion axle with trailing arms, Watt linkage, coil springs and Koni shock absorbers

Brakes: Vented discs, 11.5-in. dia. (front), 10.4-in. dia. (rear)

Wheels: Alloy, 8 x 16 in.

Tires: Goodyear Eagle, 255/50 VR16

DIMENSIONS

Length: 173.5 in. **Width:** 73.5 in.

Height: 51.1 in. **Wheelbase:** 103.2 in.

Track: 60.1 in. (front), 60.8 in. (rear)

Weight: 3,630 lbs.

Audi **RS2**

BMW has its M series, Mercedes its E500, but the magic digits for Audi were RS2. This station wagon was the ultimate wolf in sheep's clothing: an ultra high-performance car with turbocharging and four-wheel drive.

"...staggering station wagon."

"The RS2 was built with two strictly met objectives—high performance and practicality. With 315 bhp, its turbocharged 2.2-liter will dispense with a Ferrari Testarossa and leave a Porsche 911 floundering. On the practical side, this staggering station wagon is also able to take the family on a long distance road trip in perfect comfort. The all-wheel drive provides plenty of grip, and there's totally neutral handling. Not bad for a fully functional station wagon."

Bucket seats and white-faced gauges hint at the RS2's rocket-like performance.

Milestones

1992 The S2 Avant is launched: a 230-bhp turbocharged version of Audi's station wagon.

The performance S2 Avant boasted 230 bhp.

1993 An even more powerful and desirable RS2 model is launched at the Frankfurt Motor Show.

Audi's current performance wagon is the S4 Quattro Avant with a 265-bhp turbocharged V6.

1995 As the Audi A4 Avant becomes available and Audi presents a more rational model range, the RS2 is dropped along with other models in the old-style lineup.

UNDER THE SKIN

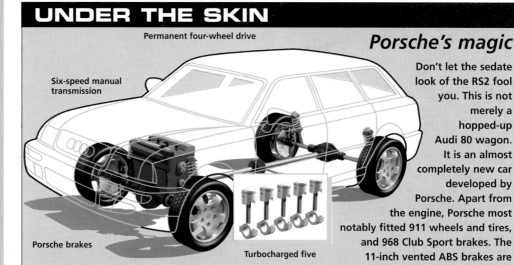

Permanent four-wheel drive

Six-speed manual transmission

Porsche brakes

Turbocharged five

Porsche's magic

Don't let the sedate look of the RS2 fool you. This is not merely a hopped-up Audi 80 wagon. It is an almost completely new car developed by Porsche. Apart from the engine, Porsche most notably fitted 911 wheels and tires, and 968 Club Sport brakes. The 11-inch vented ABS brakes are assisted by a hydraulic booster. Porsche also tweaked the suspension and included race-specified anti-roll bars and Bilstein shocks.

THE POWER PACK

Totally turbo

Audi pioneered the use of five-cylinder inline engines as early as 1978 as a successful halfway house between four- and six-cylinder units. In the RS2, that format reached its ultimate conclusion. Audi had used turbochargers before, of course, but none like the KKK's competition turbo capable of building 16 psi of boost. The modifications from the 230-bhp S2 engine include a larger intercooler, high-flow air filter, new injectors, Porsche 911 fuel pump and high-lift camshafts. Add in a low-pressure exhaust manifold and Audi was understandably happy about the figures: 315 bhp and 302 lb-ft.

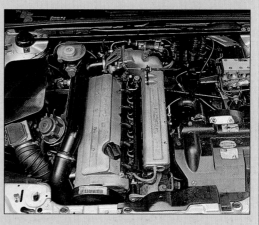

Fastest ever

As the fastest car ever made by Audi, the RS2 has an enviable reputation. In the long term, it might even eclipse the legendary Quattro as the Audi to own. Certainly, the few examples produced are highly prized by enthusiasts and rarely come up for sale—a good indication that collectors like them too much to part with them.

A Porsche heritage and serious performance guarantee exclusivity.

Audi **RS2**

Speedier and more capable than the legendary short-wheelbase Quattro Sport, the RS2 is the fastest car Audi has made. The Porsche effect is evident everywhere.

Sports interior

Audi did not forget about upgrading the cabin on its wicked wagon. Black-on-white gauges, Recaro seats and Kevlar or wood trim were added to the normal-issue Audi 80 interior. Standard equipment on the RS2 includes a power roof, power windows, CD changer and air conditioning.

Six-speed transmission

To make the most of its awesome power, Audi specified a six-speed manual transmission tweaked by Porsche. Its ratios are chosen to keep the power band around 3,000 rpm.

Porsche wheels

The elegance of the five-spoke alloy wheels should come as no surprise, as they were taken straight from the Porsche 911. They are fitted with ultra-low-profile Dunlop tires.

Practical station wagon body

The only bodystyle offered was an Avant station wagon. For such a high-performance car, this was effectively unique.

All-wheel drive

All four wheels are driven permanently by a well-proven system. It incorporates a central Torsen-type differential.

Specifications
1994 Audi RS2

ENGINE
Type: Inline five-cylinder
Construction: Cast-iron block and aluminum head
Valve gear: Four valves per cylinder operated by twin overhead camshafts
Bore and stroke: 3.19 in. x 3.40 in.
Displacement: 2,226 cc
Compression ratio: 9.0:1
Induction system: Sequential fuel injection
Maximum power: 315 bhp at 6,500 rpm
Maximum torque: 302 lb-ft at 3,000 rpm

TRANSMISSION
Six-speed manual

BODY/CHASSIS
Unitary monocoque construction with steel five-door station wagon body

SPECIAL FEATURES

The rear lights extend around onto the tailgate.

The larger, red brake calipers come from the Porsche parts bin and are from the 968 model.

RUNNING GEAR
Steering: Rack-and-pinion
Front suspension: Struts with coil springs, shock absorbers and anti-roll bar
Rear suspension: Struts with torsion beam axle, coil springs, shock absorbers and anti-roll bar
Brakes: Vented discs (front and rear)
Wheels: Alloy, 17-in. dia.
Tires: 245/40 ZR17

DIMENSIONS
Length: 177.5 in. **Width:** 66.7 in.
Height: 54.6 in. **Wheelbase:** 100.4 in.
Track: 57.0 in. (front), 57.9 in. (rear)
Weight: 3,510 lbs.

Bizzarrini **GT STRADA**

Giotto Bizzarrini—the designer of the Ferrari 250 GTO—left Ferrari to do his own thing. Racing was his passion but he also built some road cars, of which the GT Strada 5300 is the most fearsome. Its Chevy V8 engine, dramatic body and stripped-out cabin testify to that.

"...an untamed steed."

"Since it measures just 43 inches from floor to roof, your first problem is getting in. Once you're there, you can enjoy the V8 engine's gorgeous rasp—few Chevy small-blocks sound quite this loud or urgent. The GT Strada shoots off the line at a tremendous pace and has an uncanny ability to go around corners; the handling balance is one of the best of any 1960s car. This is an untamed steed that really wants to be let loose on the race track."

The compact cabin has the ambience of a race car simply decked out for road use.

Milestones

1963 At the Turin Motor Show,
Bizzarrini presents his Iso Grifo A3C competition coupe as the racing version of the Iso Grifo. It is almost identical, but lighter and lower.

Giotto Bizzarrini was involved in the design of the Ferrari 250 GTO.

1964 The A3C comes 14th in
the 24 Hours of Le Mans and wins its class.

1965 The production roadgoing
version—the GT Strada 5300—arrives.

The GT Strada 5300 was built like a race car.

1967 A smaller Opel GT-engined
model, called the Europa, is launched. Only a small number are sold.

1969 Bizzarrini ends its
days as a car manufacturer.

UNDER THE SKIN

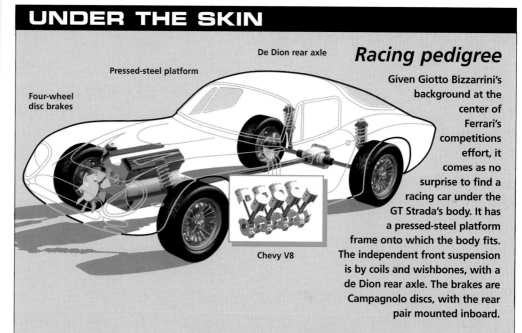

De Dion rear axle

Pressed-steel platform

Four-wheel disc brakes

Chevy V8

Racing pedigree

Given Giotto Bizzarrini's background at the center of Ferrari's competitions effort, it comes as no surprise to find a racing car under the GT Strada's body. It has a pressed-steel platform frame onto which the body fits. The independent front suspension is by coils and wishbones, with a de Dion rear axle. The brakes are Campagnolo discs, with the rear pair mounted inboard.

THE POWER PACK

Chevy power

Bizzarrini followed the practice of his former collaborator, Renzo Rivolta of Italian sports car maker Iso, in choosing Chevrolet V8 power. The 327-cubic inch cast-iron Corvette V8 was a perfect choice: very powerful, readily available and not too expensive. Early examples are tuned to 365 bhp, but most cars were supplied with a near-stock 350-bhp unit with hydraulic lifters and a compression ratio of 11.0:1. In the U.S., the standard carburetor choice was a single Holley four-barrel, but 400-bhp competition models use four carbs.

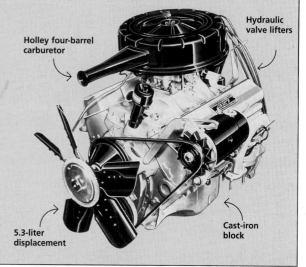

Holley four-barrel carburetor

Hydraulic valve lifters

5.3-liter displacement

Cast-iron block

GT purity

Unless you can locate one of Bizzarrini's ultra-rare racers, the GT Strada 5300 is the ultimate car bearing Giotto Bizzarrini's name. In many ways it is a purer and more focused GT car than most 1960s Ferraris, and as a classic it is an interesting choice.

The Bizzarrini makes an interesting alternative to mainstream supercars.

Bizzarrini GT STRADA

Evolved as the racing version of the Iso Grifo, the Strada's dramatic body, racing chassis and powerful engine made an intoxicating brew. For a while in the 1960s, Bizzarrini looked like a major force in the supercar stakes.

Corvette V8

The 327-cubic inch Corvette V8 engine was a logical choice for Bizzarrini, who had worked around this powerplant in the Iso Grifo (which he engineered). It was offered in near-standard specification.

Three fuel tanks

The GT Strada is a thirsty car, so to prevent constant fuel stops no less than three fuel tanks are fitted. There are two 7.5-gallon tanks in the rocker panels and a 20-gallon tank behind the seats, giving a total of 35 gallons.

Giugiaro design

The stunning shape was drawn up by a youthful Giorgetto Giugiaro while he was still working with Bertone. It was even more dramatic than the closely related Iso Grifo, also styled by Giugiaro. At just 44 inches high, it made a very strong impression.

Fiberglass bodywork

Apart from the earliest cars, which have aluminum bodywork built by Italian artisans, the bodywork is made of fiberglass. This keeps weight and costs down and makes manufacturing simpler. For competition use you could even specify thinner fiberglass body work with larger wheel openings.

Cast-alloy wheels

The evocative Campagnolo magnesium alloy wheels with knock-off center spinners look extremely purposeful. For competition use, it could be ordered with even wider rims (7 inches front and 9 inches rear).

Stripped-out cockpit

True to this car's racing roots, the cabin is not very luxurious. Two narrow bucket seats nestle between the wide sills and transmission tunnel, and the trim is minimal.

Specifications

1966 Bizzarrini GT Strada 5300

ENGINE

Type: V8

Construction: Cast-iron block and heads

Valve gear: Two valves per cylinder operated by a single camshaft with pushrods and rockers

Bore and stroke: 4.00 in. x 3.25 in.

Displacement: 327 c.i.

Compression ratio: 11.0:1

Induction system: Single Holley four-barrel carburetor

Maximum power: 365 bhp at 6,200 rpm

Maximum torque: 344 lb-ft at 4,000 rpm

TRANSMISSION

Four-speed manual

BODY/CHASSIS

Separate pressed-steel chassis with two-door coupe body

SPECIAL FEATURES

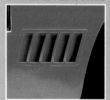

Ducts behind the front wheels carry hot air away from the cramped engine compartment.

The headlights are concealed behind plastic shrouds.

RUNNING GEAR

Steering: Recirculating ball

Front suspension: Wishbones with coil springs, shock absorbers and anti-roll bar

Rear suspension: De Dion axle with trailing arms, Watt linkage, coil springs and shock absorbers

Brakes: Discs (front and rear)

Wheels: Alloy, 15-in. dia.

Tires: Dunlop, 6.00 x 15 in. (front), 7.00 x 15 in. (rear)

DIMENSIONS

Length: 172.0 in.   **Width:** 68.0 in.

Height: 44.7 in.   **Wheelbase:** 96.5 in.

Track: 55.5 in. (front), 56.5 in. (rear)

Weight: 2,530 lbs.

Callaway CORVETTE SPEEDSTER

When turbocharging specialist Reeves Callaway built his mighty ZR-1®-beating, twin-turbo Sledgehammer version of the Corvette it was difficult to see what else could match it. The answer was the incredible and amazing-looking Corvette Speedster.

"...astounding acceleration."

"The chopped roof is disconcerting and the wraparound rear window and headrests make it difficult to see out, but practicality is not the Speedster's forté. Acceleration is astounding—it can reach 100 mph in 12.1 seconds. Callaway has reworked the Corvette suspension to increase its handling characteristics. And when you take into account the powerful brakes, enormous grip from the tires and outrageous style, the sky-high price becomes understandable."

The blue-trimmed interior is outrageous—but then so is the performance.

Milestones

1985 Reeves Callaway fits twin
turbos to an Alfa Romeo GTV6, boosting its power output to 230 bhp and taking top speed to 140 mph. Chevrolet is so impressed that it approaches Callaway to develop a twin-turbo version of the Corvette.

Callaway used the standard C4 Corvette as the basis for his turbocharged specials.

1988 Callaway produces the incredible
225-mph, 880-bhp Sledgehammer version of the Corvette. French Canadian stylist Paul Deutschman is charged with improving the stock Corvette's aerodynamics.

Callaway also has a racing program and has entered Corvettes at Le Mans.

1991 The first Speedster appears at the
Los Angeles Auto Show, and is the first car identified purely as a Callaway. The reception is amazing and Callaway prepares to make the Speedster a special edition; only 50 are built.

UNDER THE SKIN

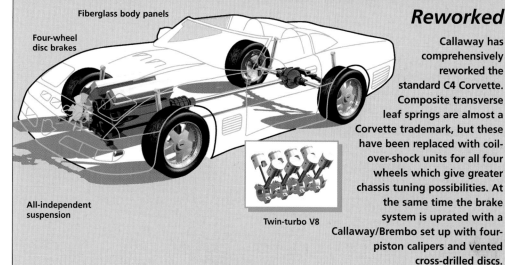

Fiberglass body panels

Four-wheel disc brakes

All-independent suspension

Twin-turbo V8

Reworked

Callaway has comprehensively reworked the standard C4 Corvette. Composite transverse leaf springs are almost a Corvette trademark, but these have been replaced with coil-over-shock units for all four wheels which give greater chassis tuning possibilities. At the same time the brake system is uprated with a Callaway/Brembo set up with four-piston calipers and vented cross-drilled discs.

THE POWER PACK

Totally revised

Callaway completely stripped and rebuilt the Corvette 350-cubic inch L98 V8, fitting a stronger crankshaft which is made from forged steel rather than cast iron. The compression ratio has been lowered to 7.5:1 using Cosworth or Mahle pistons to allow for turbocharging with twin RotoMaster turbos. The aluminum-alloy heads are milled and have stronger valve springs plus stainless-steel valves, and the standard electronic fuel injection has been recalibrated to help boost the new power output.

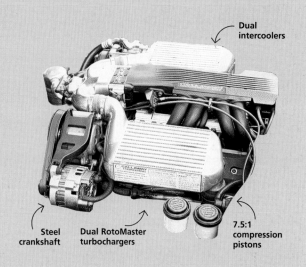

Dual intercoolers

Steel crankshaft

Dual RotoMaster turbochargers

7.5:1 compression pistons

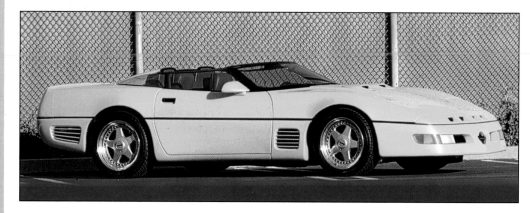

Dream Vette®

With its incredible acceleration, superior handling and braking, plus outrageous style and very limited production, the Callaway Corvette Speedster ranks among the most desirable performance car ever built, anywhere.

Only a select few are lucky enough to own a Callaway Speedster.

Callaway **CORVETTE SPEEDSTER**

Callaway proved that there was no need to go down the ZR-1 route with a complex quad-cam, 32-valve V8. It showed that all you need for huge horsepower is twin intercooled turbochargers producing 420 bhp.

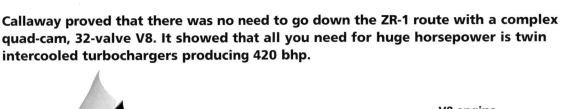

V8 engine

Callaway spent 75 hours on each stock Corvette iron-block engine, rebuilding it to exact tolerances and, with stainless-steel valves, turning it into the more powerful twin-turbo version. If the 'ordinary' 420-bhp twin-turbo unit wasn't enough, the even more powerful 450-bhp version could be bought for an extra $6,000.

Intercooled turbochargers

Most of the increase in power is due to the twin turbochargers. The watercooled RotoMaster units produce power quickly with little lag. The air is fed through twin intercoolers to keep it dense and to help release more power.

Extra vents

The Speedster features a variety of very large vents at both the front and rear to guarantee that the engine receives enough air and that the big brakes are properly cooled. Their exaggerated size is due to style as well as function.

Leather interior

Callaway would fit the very highest quality full-leather trim to the Speedster on request, but it cost an extra $12,000.

Wraparound rear window

The side glass is continued onto the rear deck and complements the prominent twin headrest humps which are a big part of the Speedster theme.

Lowered windshield

Callaway chopped seven inches from the Corvette's A-pillars to lower the windshield. However, it is not a full seven inches lower because of exaggerated rake, but it does aid aerodynamics at high speed.

Exotic colors

Speedsters were available in 12 different colors, but some of the more exotic, including Old Lyme Green, Hot Pink or Nuclear Meltdown Orange, were an expensive option at $7,500.

Specifications

1991 Callaway Corvette Speedster

ENGINE

Type: V8

Construction: Cast-iron block and alloy heads

Valve gear: Two valves per cylinder operated by a single vee-mounted camshaft via pushrods and rockers

Bore and stroke: 4.0 in. x 3.48 in.

Displacement: 350 c.i.

Compression ratio: 7.5:1

Induction system: Electronic fuel injection with Callaway Micro Fueler controller and twin RotoMaster turbochargers

Maximum power: 420 bhp at 4,250 rpm

Maximum torque: 562 lb-ft at 2,500 rpm

TRANSMISSION

Six-speed manual

BODY/CHASSIS

Separate steel chassis frame with two-seater fiberglass open speedster body

SPECIAL FEATURES

A lowered windshield prevents air from buffeting inside the cabin.

The Speedster has a special plaque mounted on the console next to the boost gauge.

RUNNING GEAR

Steering: Rack-and-pinion

Front suspension: Double wishbones with coil springs, telescopic shock absorbers and anti-roll bar

Rear suspension: Multi-link with coil springs, telescopic shock absorbers and anti-roll bar

Brakes: Brembo vented discs with four-piston calipers (front and rear)

Wheels: Alloy, 9.5 x 18 in. (front), 11 x 18 in. (rear)

Tires: Bridgestone RE71 285/35 ZR18

DIMENSIONS

Length: 176.5 in.   **Width:** 71.0 in.

Height: 39.7 in.   **Wheelbase:** 92.2 in.

Track: 59.6 in. (front), 60.4 in. (rear)

Weight: 3,200 lbs.

Chevrolet **CORVETTE ZR-1**

**With its Lotus-designed quad-cam V8 engine, the ZR-1
has a more advanced powerplant and superior performance than the current
C5 Corvette. It is the ultimate Corvette—a genuine world-class supercar.**

"...the ultimate Corvette?"

*"Above 3,500 rpm, when all 16 injectors are pumping fuel as fast as the
engine can use it, the ZR-1's performance is astounding, even for
early models. With the later 405 bhp engines there were few
cars on the road to challenge the ZR-1's performance. The chassis
easily copes with the huge power output. The ride may be harsh
and the interior cramped, but this is a supercar with sensitive
steering, powerful brakes, and fine rear-wheel drive road
manners."*

*Lateral support in the ZR-1 is excellent, although the cockpit is difficult
to enter.*

Milestones

1984 A new Corvette
is finally introduced in 1983 as a 1984 model. The fourth-generation Corvette is the best in years, but, although it retains the front-engine rear-drive format, it severely needs more power.

By 1956 the Corvette finally matured, and turned into a serious sports car.

1986 The Corvette
roadster is revived, and goes on sale this year. It is selected as a pace car for the Indianapolis 500.

1990 After much
hype, the ZR-1 finally enters production. It has unique rear end styling to distinguish it from the standard Corvette.

An all-new, fifth-generation Corvette debuted in 1997.

1993 Power is
boosted to 405 bhp and a special 40th anniversary trim package is available on all Corvettes. The ZR-1 returns for two more seasons with new five-spoke alloy wheels.

UNDER THE SKIN

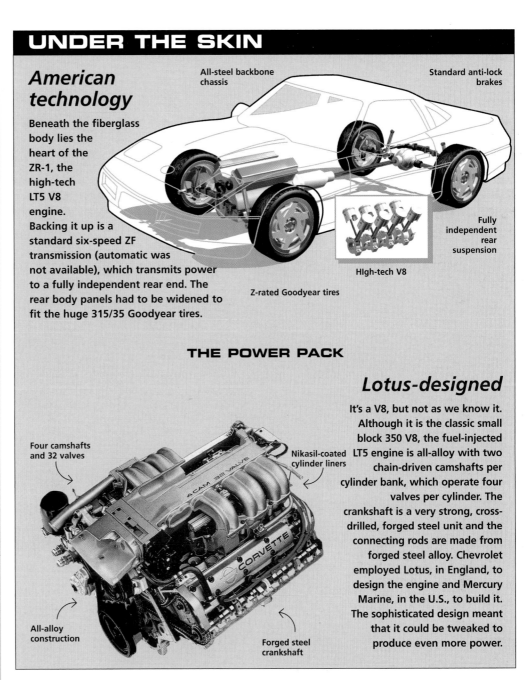

American technology

Beneath the fiberglass body lies the heart of the ZR-1, the high-tech LT5 V8 engine. Backing it up is a standard six-speed ZF transmission (automatic was not available), which transmits power to a fully independent rear end. The rear body panels had to be widened to fit the huge 315/35 Goodyear tires.

All-steel backbone chassis

Standard anti-lock brakes

Fully independent rear suspension

High-tech V8

Z-rated Goodyear tires

THE POWER PACK

Four camshafts and 32 valves

Nikasil-coated cylinder liners

All-alloy construction

Forged steel crankshaft

Lotus-designed

It's a V8, but not as we know it. Although it is the classic small block 350 V8, the fuel-injected LT5 engine is all-alloy with two chain-driven camshafts per cylinder bank, which operate four valves per cylinder. The crankshaft is a very strong, cross-drilled, forged steel unit and the connecting rods are made from forged steel alloy. Chevrolet employed Lotus, in England, to design the engine and Mercury Marine, in the U.S., to build it. The sophisticated design meant that it could be tweaked to produce even more power.

Brute force

In 1993 Chevrolet began to make use of the powerful Lotus-designed LT5 V8, pushing up its output to 405 bhp at 5,800 rpm and the torque to 385 lb-ft. The early ZR-1s may have been fast, but the extra power of the later model really makes them move.

This post-1993 model has an increased power output of 405 bhp.

Chevrolet CORVETTE ZR-1

With the ZR-1, Chevrolet proved that an exotic mid-mounted engine and $100,000 price tag are not required to offer true supercar performance.

Plastic springs
Like all Corvettes since the launch of the 1963 Coupe, the ZR-1 features transverse leaf springs. These are now made from plastic for reduced weight.

Quad-cam V8
A technological masterpiece, the LT5 was originally intended for boats. Although all-alloy, it weighs more than a cast-iron Chevy small block.

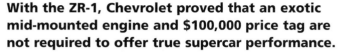

Traction control
Corvettes were often tricky to control on slippery roads. The introduction of ASR (Anti-Slip Regulation) considerably reduced the tendency for the car to slide on wet roads.

Tire-pressure monitor
For 1989 all Corvettes received a tire-pressure monitoring device which warns the driver, by means of a flashing light, if tire pressures are low.

CAGS gear selection
Computer-Aided Gear Selection (CAGS) is a device which skips shifts in low gears at light throttle openings.

Valet key

To prevent certain individuals from experiencing the ZR-1's full performance, a special key can be used to restrict horsepower.

Fiberglass bodywork

The ZR-1, like all Corvettes, retains fiberglass bodywork. The back half of the car had to be widened to fit the ZR-1s large wheels.

Selective ride control

At the touch of a switch the ZR-1 driver can select three different suspension settings: Touring, Sport, or Performance. As speed increases, the shocks are stiffened by a computer that is able to make 10 adjustments per second.

Variable fuel injection

During normal driving, the ZR-1's engine uses only eight primary ports and injectors. With the throttle floored and the engine turning above 3,500 rpm, the eight secondary injectors are brought into action, producing truly awesome performance.

Specifications
1991 Chevrolet Corvette ZR-1

ENGINE
Type: LT5 V8
Construction: Alloy block, heads and cylinder liners
Valve gear: Four valves per cylinder operated by four overhead camshafts
Bore and stroke: 3.90 in. x 3.66 in.
Displacement: 350 c.i.
Compression ratio: 11:1
Induction system: Multi-port fuel injection
Maximum power: 375 bhp at 5,800 rpm
Maximum torque: 371 lb-ft at 4,800 rpm

TRANSMISSION
ZF six-speed manual

BODY/CHASSIS
Separate steel chassis with fiberglass two-door coupe body

SPECIAL FEATURES

A unique feature of the LT5 is the three-stage throttle control.

Prototype ZR-1s retained the original 1984 instrument panel layout.

RUNNING GEAR
Steering: Rack-and-pinion
Front suspension: Double wishbones, transverse plastic leaf springs, and telescopic adjustable shocks
Rear suspension: Upper and lower trailing links, transverse plastic leaf spring, telescopic adjustable shocks, and anti-roll bar
Brakes: Vented discs front and rear, 13 in. dia. (front), 12 in. dia. (rear)
Wheels: Alloy, 17 x 9.5-in. dia. (front), 17 x 11-in. dia. (rear)
Tires: Goodyear Eagle ZR40, 275/40 ZR17 (front), 315/35 ZR17 (rear)

DIMENSIONS
Length: 178.5 in.   **Width:** 73.2 in.
Height: 46.7 in.
Wheelbase: 96.2 in.
Track: 60 in. (front), 62 in. (rear)
Weight: 3,519 lbs.

De Tomaso **MANGUSTA**

De Tomaso's first volume production sports car was a mid-engined, supercar designed to challenge Ferrari. It paved the way for the famous Pantera, although in some ways its design was more advanced and more like the racing car from which it was developed.

"...a perfect combination."

"A light front end, flexible chassis and less-than-perfect driving position ensure the Mangusta is a challenge. Against that, there's a perfect combination of power and torque, giving all the performance its shape promises; 100 mph comes up in an impressive 18.7 seconds. The steering is light and the straight line stability good, but don't throw this car into bends too hard; mid-engined cars, particularly this one, don't like it. "

The fully-equipped dashboard gives the Mangusta a strong race car feel.

Milestones

1965 The Turin Motor Show

sees an open mid-engined racer, the 70P, appear. It has a central backbone much like De Tomaso's Vallelunga road car, but a 5.0-liter Ford engine rather than a 1.5-liter. It is styled by an ex-GM designer, Pete Brock, and built by coachbuilders Fantuzzi.

Conceived in the early 1960s, the Vallelunga was ahead of its time.

1966 The basic structure

of the 70P reappears at the next Turin Show, now covered by the stylish Giugiaro-designed body.

1967 Production of the Mangusta

begins with the one-of-a-kind fiberglass show body replaced by sheet metal and aluminum.

The Pantera was built in greater numbers than the Mangusta.

1971 Production ceases

after 400 Mangustas (including one convertible) have been made. About 300 were exported to the U.S.

UNDER THE SKIN

Racing heritage

Technically more advanced than the later and more famous Pantera, the Mangusta has a folded and welded sheet steel box-section central backbone. Onto the back of that is mounted the Ford V8 acting, as in a racing car, as a stressed chassis member. Right at the back is the ZF five-speed transmission with long shifter linkage. The classic racing car suspension has double wishbones at the front and rear.

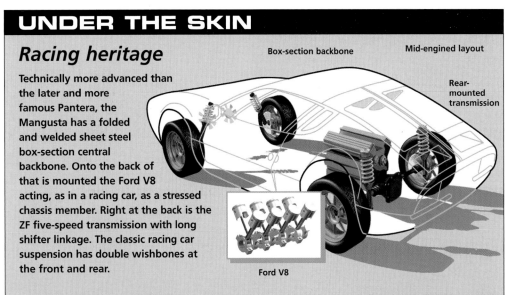

Box-section backbone

Mid-engined layout

Rear-mounted transmission

Ford V8

THE POWER PACK

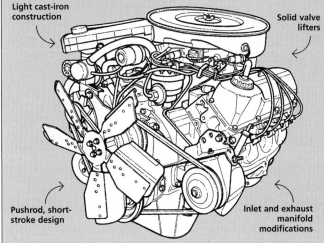

Light cast-iron construction

Solid valve lifters

Pushrod, short-stroke design

Inlet and exhaust manifold modifications

Modified Fords

De Tomaso used two Ford engines, the 289 and 302. Both are essentially the same and share a surprisingly light cast-iron pushrod, short-stroke V8 design. The HiPo 289 with its stronger connecting rods, higher compression ratio and solid rather than hydraulic valve lifters is the unit used in the fast Mustangs, AC Cobras and the Shelby GT350. De Tomaso decided to have the same modifications as Shelby, using improved intake and exhaust manifolds to make the engine breathe better.

Euro models

Curiously for a car intended for the U.S., the European-spec Mangusta is the one to choose as it has the 289 V8 with 305 bhp compared with 230 bhp from a larger 302. Naturally, the Euro spec cars have quicker acceleration and a higher top speed, too.

European-spec versions are more powerful than those built for the U.S.

De Tomaso MANGUSTA

This is now one of the forgotten supercars, but it would have been a very different story if De Tomaso had given the powerful Mangusta the development its stunning Giugiaro design merited.

Glass engine covers

Giugiaro's solution to engine access was to design two transparent covers which opened up, pivoting from the center. They are an impressive sight when up, but access is awkward nevertheless.

V8 engine

Given De Tomaso's close links with Ford (the later Pantera was a joint Ford/De Tomaso enterprise), it was no surprise that De Tomaso chose to use the 289- and 302-cubic inch Ford V8s. They give plenty of power and are very reliable.

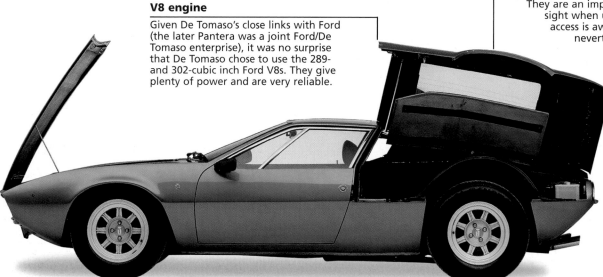

Front radiator

Although De Tomaso mounted the radiator at the front and ran pipes back to the engine to offset the car's weight distribution, the Mangusta was still very rear-heavy.

Rear-biased weight distribution

A combination of the all-iron V8, clutch, final drive and heavy ZF transmission at the back of the car gives the Mangusta a very heavy rear weight bias—as much as 68 percent of the weight at the back.

Giugiaro styling

After he moved on from Bertone, Giorgetto Giugiaro was, for a time, head of styling at Ghia (then owned by De Tomaso). During this time, he designed the body for the Mangusta. It still looks stunning today, more than thirty years after its debut.

Bigger rear tires

With the weight at the back of the car the front and rear tires are different sizes, with 185 HR15s at the front and 225 HR15s at the rear. Time has proven that the car needs even larger, more modern tires for its performance to be safely exploited.

Alloy hood

Strangely, given that the Mangusta's design ensures that it is light at the front, it has an alloy hood which makes the problem worse.

Specifications

1970 De Tomaso Mangusta

ENGINE

Type: V8

Construction: Cast-iron block and heads

Valve gear: Two valves per cylinder operated by single V-mounted camshafts via pushrods and rockers

Bore and stroke: 4.00 in. x 3.00 in.

Displacement: 4,950 cc

Compression ratio: 10.0:1

Induction system: Four-barrel carburetor

Maximum power: 230 bhp at 4,800 rpm

Maximum torque: 310 lb-ft at 2,800 rpm

TRANSMISSION

Rear-mounted ZF five-speed manual

BODY/CHASSIS

Sheet steel backbone chassis with engine and transmission as stressed members and alloy and steel two-door coupe body

SPECIAL FEATURES

By way of a nod to Ferrari, the Mangusta has a gated shifter.

The triple line engine vents on the C-pillars are a neat styling touch.

RUNNING GEAR

Steering: Rack-and-pinion

Front suspension: Double wishbones with coil springs, telescopic shock absorbers and anti-roll bar

Rear suspension: Reversed lower wishbone with single transverse link and twin radius arms per side, coil springs, telescopic shock absorbers and anti-roll bar

Brakes: Girling discs, 11.5-in. dia. (front), 11.0-in. dia. (rear)

Wheels: Magnesium alloy, 7 x 15 in. (front), 7.5 x 15 in. (rear)

Tires: 185 HR15 (front), 225 HR15 (rear)

DIMENSIONS

Length: 168.3 in.   **Width:** 72.0 in.

Height: 43.3 in.   **Wheelbase:** 98.4 in.

Track: 54.9 in. (front), 57.1 in. (rear)

Weight: 2,915 lbs.

De Tomaso PANTERA

The combination of an exotic Italian-styled body with the strength, power and reliability of a huge American V8 engine seemed to offer the best of both worlds to some manufacturers, De Tomaso in particular. The Pantera is one of the world's longest-lived supercars.

"Acceleration is shattering."

"That massive engine thunders away just behind your head, shaking the whole car and generating enough heat to make the standard air conditioning absolutely vital. Shifts are made with the ZF 5-speed transaxle, steering is light and handling impressive. The grip on those huge tires is enormous and the Pantera rides flat through the sharpest of turns. Its 5.6-second 0-60 acceleration is shattering and 165 mph top speed is virtually unmatched by any competitor. In fact, the exotic Italian-styled car looks fast even when it's standing still."

The Pantera interior has plush leather seats and instruments that are very easy to see.

Milestones

1969 Ford provides funds to produce the first Pantera. De Tomaso retains European sales rights, while Ford retains the rights in the U.S.

1971 Pantera goes on sale.

The Mangusta was De Tomaso's first V8-engined supercar.

1974 Chassis revisions, better brakes and a 330-bhp 351 'Cleveland' Ford V8 engine are in the European-spec GTS models. Due to emissions regulations, U.S. models produce only 266 bhp. Ford pulls out of the project leaving De Tomaso to build the cars independently.

1982 The GT5 is launched. Tacked-on wheel arch extensions are used to fit wider wheels and tires.

The GT5 gained wheel arch extensions and rear spoiler.

1990 Dramatic revamp is undertaken, although the concept stays the same. The engine is now Ford's popular 5.0 liter that makes 305 bhp with natural aspiration. By adding twin turbochargers, the Pantera makes up to 450 bhp.

UNDER THE SKIN

Mighty monocoque

Unusual for an Italian supercar, the Pantera has a steel monocoque structure. The car was planned to be sold in high volume through Ford dealers, so a separate chassis design would have been too labor-intensive and slow. The big Ford V8 is mounted behind the driver, turning the rear wheels through a rugged ZF five-speed transaxle. Double-wishbone suspension is used on all four wheels.

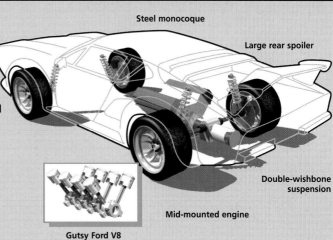

Steel monocoque

Large rear spoiler

Double-wishbone suspension

Mid-mounted engine

Gutsy Ford V8

THE POWER PACK

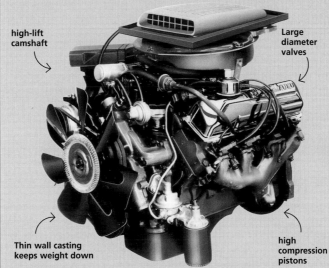

high-lift camshaft

Large diameter valves

Thin wall casting keeps weight down

high compression pistons

Ford power

The best engine to be fitted to the Pantera was the Ford 'Cleveland' V8 (named after the plant where it was built). It is a conventional all-iron V8 with high-lift camshaft and hydraulic lifters, although solid lifters could be specified for higher rpm. Although big, at 5,763 cc, its thin wall casting made it relatively lightweight. The engine could easily be tuned to produce more power with a high compression ratio, big valves, higher lift cams, free-flowing exhaust systems and multiple carburetors rather than one Holley.

1990s Pantera

The Pantera was totally updated for the 90s with the introduction of the Gandini-styled 450 in 1990. It uses twin turbochargers to boost the power of a smaller 5.0-liter V8 engine to 450 bhp, hence the name. De Tomaso claims a top speed over 180 mph.

Gandini's restyle and twin turbos really brought the Pantera up to date.

De Tomaso PANTERA

The Pantera was built tough to survive on the U.S. market, with a simple and strong Ford V8 engine. It proved to be the right approach and the Pantera stayed in production long after it should have become obsolete.

Wishbone suspension

The Pantera featured double-wishbone suspension with telescopic shocks, coil springs and anti-roll bars.

Five-speed transaxle

To better handle the power output of the V8 engine, a strong ZF five-speed transaxle was used, along with a limited slip differential.

Steel monocoque

As it was intended to be built in large numbers for a supercar (Ford hoped for 5,000 a year), it was designed to be built like a mass-production car, with a unitary steel monocoque.

Ford V8 engine

Because the Pantera was to be sold through Ford in the large U.S. market, it used a Ford Cleveland 5,763 cc V8 overhead valve engine design that was used in many early Mustangs.

Front spoiler

Designed to complement that flamboyant extrovert rear wing, the front spoiler plays its part in cutting down the amount of air that can flow under the car.

Carbon fiber rear spoiler

A rear spoiler was optional on the Pantera to provide extra downforce at very high speeds. By the 1980s that spoiler was made of carbon fiber.

Unequal-size wheels

To carry the large rear tires the rear wheels are 13 inches wide, compared with the slimmer 10-inch wide front wheels.

Extra driving lights

Its headlights were never the Pantera's strong suit and the extra driving lights which could be fitted in front of the air dam were a valuable addition.

Specifications
1986 De Tomaso Pantera GT5S

ENGINE

Type: Ford V8
Construction: Cast-iron block and heads
Valve gear: Two valves per cylinder operated by single block-mounted camshaft via pushrods and rockers
Bore and stroke: 4.01 in. x 3.50 in.
Displacement: 5,763 cc
Compression ratio: 10.5:1
Induction system: Single four-barrel Holley 680 cfm carburetor
Maximum power: 350 bhp at 6,000 rpm
Maximum torque: 451 lb-ft at 3,800 rpm

TRANSMISSION

ZF five-speed manual transaxle

BODY/CHASSIS

Steel monocoque two-door, two-seat coupe

SPECIAL FEATURES

Wheel vents in the rear arch extensions redirect cool air to the brakes keeping them from getting too hot and fading at high speeds.

Like the Lamborghini Countach, De Tomaso Panteras came with an optional rear spoiler. It was as much for style as function.

RUNNING GEAR

Steering: Rack-and-pinion
Front suspension: Double wishbones with coil springs, telescopic shocks and anti-roll bar
Rear suspension: Double wishbones, coil springs, telescopic shocks and anti-roll bar
Brakes: 11.7 in. discs (front) vented 11.2 in. discs (rear)
Wheels: Alloy,10 in. x 15 in. (front), 13 in. x 15 in. (rear)
Tires: 285/40 VR15 (front), 345/35 VR15 (rear)

DIMENSIONS

Length: 168.1 in.   **Width:** 77.5 in.
Wheelbase: 99 in.   **Height:** 44.3 in.
Track: 61 in. (front), 62.1 in. (rear)
Weight: 3,202 lbs.

Dodge VIPER GTS-R

The Viper GTS had such a good platform that it cried out to be turned into a racing car. And in GT2 racing, the GTS-R, with its 650-bhp V10, has consistently beaten the best and won its class at the 24 Hours of Le Mans.

"...a raging animal."

"Climb in this raging animal and prepare for the ride of your life. Nail the throttle and dump the clutch and feel yourself catapult to 60 mph in a staggering 3.1 seconds. The thrill doesn't stop there though. This scorching Dodge continues to pull hard through all perfectly matched gears until it reaches its terminal velocity at just over 200 mph. Jam on the massive brakes and you will find that the GTS-R's stopping performance matches its astounding acceleration."

With five-point harnesses and white-faced gauges this Viper is ready to bite.

Milestones

1995 Chrysler
startles viewers in Pebble Beach, California by unveiling its proposed racing version of the hardtop Dodge Viper GTS.

Dodge launched the Viper in 1991, with the RT/10.

1996 Dodge
actually takes the GTS-R racing as promised.

1997 Sensibly,
Chrysler focuses on the GT2 category in world sportscar racing. It finishes 1-2 in class at the Le Mans 24 Hours. The GTS-R takes the World GT2 championship overall, a first for an American production model. English GTS-R driver Justin Bell takes the driver's championship.

Viper driver Justin Bell (right) celebrates after winning the 1998 24 Hours of Le Mans.

1998 To celebrate
its stunning achievements, Dodge offers the GTS-R on sale to the public, on a limited basis.

UNDER THE SKIN

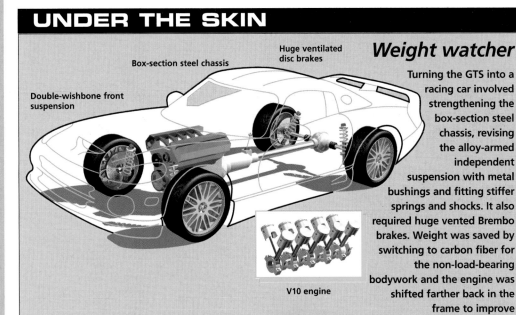

Box-section steel chassis

Huge ventilated disc brakes

Double-wishbone front suspension

V10 engine

Weight watcher

Turning the GTS into a racing car involved strengthening the box-section steel chassis, revising the alloy-armed independent suspension with metal bushings and fitting stiffer springs and shocks. It also required huge vented Brembo brakes. Weight was saved by switching to carbon fiber for the non-load-bearing bodywork and the engine was shifted farther back in the frame to improve weight distribution.

THE POWER PACK

Reworked V10

This engine is nothing like the standard Viper powerplant. For the racing GTS-R, Dodge seriously reworked the all-alloy 8-liter Ferrari eater V10 to give 650 bhp. It is still a single-cam, pushrod engine, but the fully balanced and blueprinted engine benefits from a 12.0:1 compression ratio and stronger forged steel connecting rods. Extensive work is done to both the intake and exhaust systems to extract maximum power. A dry sump oiling system prevents oil from surging when the car takes turns at high speeds. Maximum power is a massive 650 bhp at 6,500 rpm.

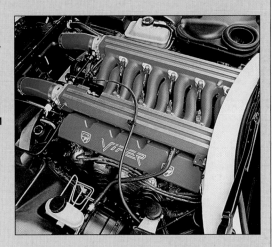

Track racer

The GTS-R is a rare model. It has outrageous power at 650 bhp, along with carbon-fiber bodywork, stripped racing interior with digital dashboard meter and a real racing suspension. Of course, a racetrack is needed to get the most out of it.

In GT2, the Vipers have proven almost unbeatable.

Dodge VIPER GTS-R

Dodge stunned the world when it decided to produce the RT/10 in 1991. It then went on to impress hard-core endurance racing enthusiasts when it took the FIA championship in the GT2 class in its fully outfitted GTS-R race car.

V10 engine

The roadgoing versions of the GTS-R, now known as the ACR, do get more power from their V10s, but nowhere near the 650 bhp of the racers. However, 460 bhp at 5,200 rpm is more than respectable.

Composite body

Composite paneling is used for the street GTS-R, just as it is in the usual GTS, but for the serious racing cars the bodywork was made from lightweight carbon fiber.

Front airdam

The GT2 rules allow some bodywork revision in aid of improved aerodynamics. This explains the GTS-R's different, deeper nose and rocker panel extensions. These modifications keep air away from the underside of the car, where it can generate drag and lift.

Adjustable pedals

The ideal driving position is vital in any performance car such as the GTS-R. To help achieve this, electronically controlled foot pedals let the driver get the right relationship between the pedals and steering wheel.

Multilink rear suspension

Rear suspension design is an SLA design with adjustable toe link. Similar to the front suspension the rubber bushings are replaced by spherical bearings and the springs and shocks are all stiffened.

Specifications

1997 Dodge Viper GTS-R

ENGINE
Type: V10

Construction: Alloy block and heads

Valve gear: Two valves per cylinder operated by a single V-mounted camshaft with pushrods and rockers

Bore and stroke: 4.00 in. x 3.88 in.

Displacement: 8.0 Liter

Compression ratio: 12.0:1

Induction system: Electronic fuel injection

Maximum power: 650 bhp at 6,000 rpm

Maximum torque: 650 lb-ft at 5,000 rpm

TRANSMISSION
Borg-Warner six-speed manual

BODY/CHASSIS
Separate steel box-section chassis with either carbon-fiber or glass-fiber two-door coupe body

SPECIAL FEATURES

With a sure-shifting six speed, it is easy to row through the gears in a Viper GTS-R.

The twin tailpipes help the GTS-R to produce a fantastic exhaust note.

RUNNING GEAR
Steering: Rack-and-pinion

Front suspension: SLA with coil springs, telescopic shock absorbers, spherical bearings and anti-roll bar

Rear suspension: SLA with extra toe-adjustment link, coil springs, telescopic shocks and anti-roll bar

Brakes: Ventilated discs, 13.0-in. dia.

Wheels: Alloy, 18 x 11(F), BB5 3-piece 18 x 13(rear)

Tires: Michelin Pilot SX Radial Slicks 27/65-18(front), 30/80-18(rear)

DIMENSIONS
Length: 176.7 in. **Width:** 75.7 in.

Height: 45.1 in. **Wheelbase:** 96.2 in.

Track: 59.8 in. (front), 60.9 in. (rear)

Weight: 2,750 lbs.

Ferrari 288 GTO

Gran Turismo Omologato (GTO) signifies a production car which has been sanctioned to race. In 1984 Ferrari resurrected the name for its latest twin-turbo supercar. In all, 271 were built to qualify for Group B endurance racing.

"...reminiscent of the 1960s GTO."

On first acquaintance, the GTO is not for everyone—especially someone expecting a comfortable ride. It is reminiscent of the 1960s GTO—cramped, noisy, hard-riding, with a tight shifter and a stiff clutch. Take it out on a highway, however, and it really comes into its own. The turbocharged V8 catapults the GTO to 60 mph in just 5.0 seconds and handling is sensational—a near-perfect blend of power-off understeer and power-on oversteer."

Unlike the F40, the 288 GTO is quite lavish, with leather seats and wind-down windows.

Milestones

1984 At the launch of the 288 GTO
at the Geneva Motor Show, Ferrari announces that just 200 cars will be built.

The original 250 GTO made its racing debut at Sebring in 1962.

1985 Demand proves so high
that Ferrari reluctantly has to expand production beyond the intended 200 cars.

After Group B is cancelled, Ferrari used the technology from the 288 GTO as the basis for the F40.

1987 The final GTO is delivered
to two-time F1 World Champion Niki Lauda. By this time, values of used examples have soared much higher than their list price. To commemorate the 40th anniversary of the firm, Ferrari builds a special batch of F40s that are based on the GTO chassis and running gear. It is the first road car to exceed 200 mph.

UNDER THE SKIN

Classic Ferrari

Essentially, the 288 GTO is based on the 308 GTB chassis and shares its basic layout of a multi-tubular frame, all-independent suspension and steel body styling. In true racing style, the engine is positioned longitudinally, rather than transversely as in the 308 GTB, and a new five-speed transaxle is mounted behind it. This results in a stretch to 96 inches between the wheel centers; the track is also widened by 4 inches. The bodywork is built from composite materials.

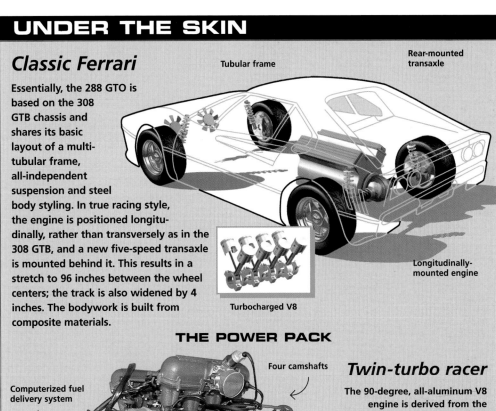

Tubular frame

Rear-mounted transaxle

Longitudinally-mounted engine

Turbocharged V8

THE POWER PACK

Computerized fuel delivery system

Four camshafts

Twin IHI turbochargers

Aluminum block and cylinder heads

Twin-turbo racer

The 90-degree, all-aluminum V8 engine is derived from the 'quattrovalvolve' unit used in the 308 GTB. It is strengthened in many areas and reduced in size to comply with regulations which stated a maximum capacity of 4.0 liters. Two separate fuel injection/ignition systems are fitted, one for each bank of four cylinders. To eliminate turbo-lag, two small IHI intercooled turbochargers are used, resulting in 400 bhp at a maximum turbo boost of 11.8 psi.

All-time great

As a limited production homologation special, the 288 GTO will always have a hallowed place in the list of all-time Ferrari greats. It is beautifully understated on the surface and a proper racing machine underneath—a true thoroughbred.

As soon as production ended, the value of the 288 GTO began to rise.

Ferrari 288 GTO 🇮🇹

When the 288 GTO was launched it was the fastest car in the world and Ferrari's most radical roadgoing machine. Although it never actually raced, it paved the way for the incredible F40.

Classic Pininfarina styling

Only the most nit-picking critic could raise any objections about the near-perfect styling of the 288 GTO, which was created by Pininfarina.

Longitudinal engine

Unlike the transverse-engined 308 GTB from which the GTO is derived, the engine is positioned lengthways with the transmission mated to the end of it. The whole drivetrain is so long that the transmission endplate is clearly visible at the back of the car.

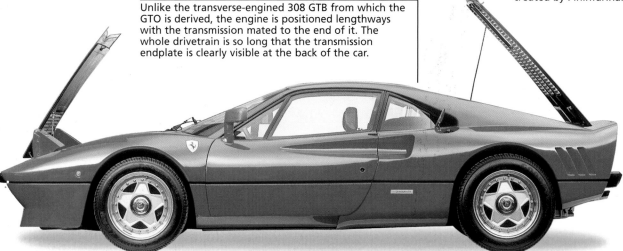

Compact independent suspension

To keep the height of the front suspension to a minimum for a low nose line, it connects to the lower end of each hub carrier and feeds loads into the structure between the wishbone mounts. At the rear, the spring/shock absorber units are attached to the top of the hub carrier because the height here is not as critical.

Unique disc brakes

The vented disc brakes for the 288 GTO were specially developed by Ferrari and Brembo. The front pair are fitted with twin-pot calipers.

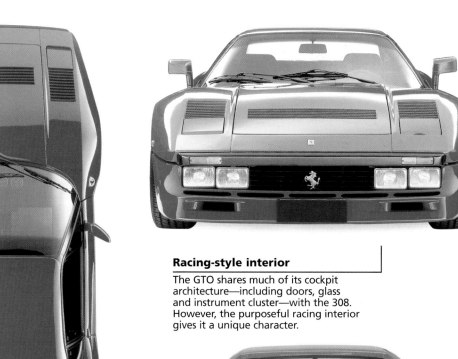

Racing-style interior

The GTO shares much of its cockpit architecture—including doors, glass and instrument cluster—with the 308. However, the purposeful racing interior gives it a unique character.

Twin-turbo power

Although its ancestry lies with the 308 GTB V8, the GTO engine was unique, with a smaller capacity but a much higher output. This is mostly due to twin IHI turbochargers with separate intercoolers, special electronic fuel injection and modified engine internals.

Specifications

1984 Ferrari 288 GTO

ENGINE

Type: V8

Construction: Aluminum block and heads

Valve gear: Four valves per cylinder operated by double overhead camshafts

Bore and stroke: 3.15 in. x 2.8 in.

Displacement: 2,855 cc

Compression ratio: 7.6:1

Induction system: Weber-Marelli electronic fuel injection

Maximum power: 394 bhp at 7,000 rpm

Maximum torque: 366 lb-ft at 3,800 rpm

TRANSMISSION

Five-speed manual

BODY/CHASSIS

Tubular-steel spaceframe clothed in composite two-door coupe body

SPECIAL FEATURES

To get maximum performance from its 2,855 cc engine, the GTO benefits from dual intercooled turbochargers.

An instant recognition feature of the GTO is its high-mounted door mirrors.

RUNNING GEAR

Steering: Rack-and-pinion

Front suspension: Unequal length wishbones with coil springs, telescopic shock absorbers and anti-roll bar

Rear suspension: Unequal length wishbones with coil springs, telescopic shock absorbers and anti-roll bar

Brakes: Vented discs (front and rear)

Wheels: Alloy, 16-in. dia

Tires: 225/50 VR16 (front), 265/50 VR16 (rear)

DIMENSIONS

Length: 168.9 in.   **Width:** 75.2 in.

Height: 44.1 in.   **Wheelbase:** 96.5 in.

Track: 61.4 in. (front) 61.5 in. (rear)

Weight: 2,880 lbs.

Ferrari 308

As the successor to the Dino, the 308 carried on the small, mid-engined Ferrari theme. However, its engine had grown from a V6 to a V8 and would end up bigger and more powerful in the 328.

"...always enough power."

"With World Champion driver Niki Lauda providing input, it's no surprise that the 308 is one of the best-handling Ferraris. It's biased toward initial slight understeer, but there's always enough power to move the tail out with the throttle. But, as with all mid-engined cars, care is needed because the transition from controlled slide into spin is sudden. At low speeds, the clutch and steering are both heavier than you expect, but the performance is just what you want. With the high-revving V8 screaming toward its limit, 0-60 mph takes just over six seconds."

The 308 GTB is a shameless two-seater, with space under the hood for only a spare wheel.

Milestones

1973 308 GT4 Dino is the first to have the 3-liter V8. Its Bertone styling is not universally praised, so Ferrari turns back to Pininfarina for the next car, the new 308 which first appears at the 1975 Paris Show.

Some 3,500 examples of the Bertone-designed GT4 Dino 2+2 sold over seven years.

1977 At the Frankfurt Show, Ferrari unveils the Targa-topped GTS model with its removable roof section.

1980 Essentially a 2+2 308, the Mondial is introduced at the Geneva Show with totally different styling from the two-seater.

Mondial was produced as a convertible as well as a coupe.

1982 To compensate for power lost through meeting emissions standards, new four-valve heads are introduced with the 'quattrovalvole' model, capable of a top speed of 152 mph.

1985 Production of the 308 ends to make way for the new 328.

UNDER THE SKIN

Ferrari traditions

The 308 has typical Ferrari construction with a separate chassis welded from square-section steel tube onto which the body was added. That was made of fiberglass initially, but was replaced by steel in 1977. The V8 engine is transversely mounted behind the cockpit just in front of the rear wheels. Its suspension is just as typically Ferrari as the chassis, with wishbones all around.

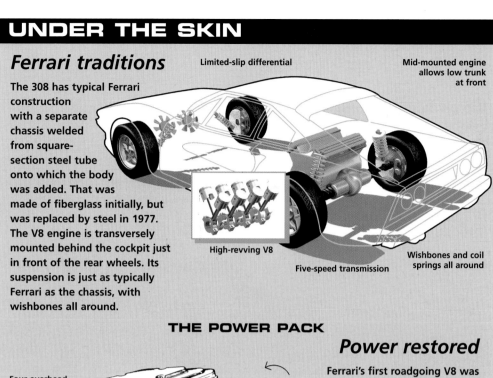

Limited-slip differential

Mid-mounted engine allows low trunk at front

High-revving V8

Five-speed transmission

Wishbones and coil springs all around

THE POWER PACK

Four overhead camshafts

Marelli ignition

First Ferrari engine with belt-driven cams

Nikasil-treated cylinders

Power restored

Ferrari's first roadgoing V8 was distantly related to the engine which gave John Surtees his World Championship in 1964. The all-alloy engine first appeared in the Dino GT4, with four belt-driven overhead cams and two valves per cylinder. Initially using carburetors, this V8 acquired fuel injection in1981, followed by 'quattrovalvole' four-valve heads in 1982. With these mechanical inventions power was restored to 240 bhp due to U.S. emissions requirements.

Ultimate GT

Although the 308 evolved into the more powerful 328, the ultimate evolution was the 288 GTO (Gran Turismo Omologato). It shares the same body style but has an extremely powerful twin-turbo V8 giving 400 bhp and a top speed of 175 mph.

The GTO was designed for Group B racing, which never reached fruition.

Ferrari 308

It's hard to imagine that the 308 shape is over 20 years old. The replacement for the little Dino is a timeless classic and its quad-cam V8 means it has the power to compliment the looks.

Radiator air vents
The hot air which passes through the front-mounted radiator is vented through these small grills on top of the fenders.

Quad-cam V8
By the time this car was built, the quad-cam Ferrari V8 had acquired two more valves per cylinder to form the 32-valve 'quattrovalvole' version.

Four-wheel vented discs
Because of its virtually even weight distribution front to rear, the 308 uses similar size discs at both ends. All are vented to provide maximum braking efficiency.

Tubular steel chassis
Some things never seem to change at Ferrari, like the separate steel tube chassis. The 308 could not have been a monocoque design; Ferrari preferred the traditional approach.

Targa top
This GTS version has a Targa-style top in which a section of the roof can be removed and stowed away under the hood. Introduced two years after the GTB, the GTS is an excellent compromise between coupe and a full convertible.

Engine air intake
One side vent guides air to the oil cooler and the other channels it to the engine's air intake—either carburetors or fuel injection, depending on the age of the car.

Pop-up headlights

Perhaps the most significant styling difference between Dino and 308 is the switch from exposed headlights to the pop-up type, which allow the flatter, sloping nose.

Fuel injection

By 1981 the traditional Weber carburetors had been replaced by Bosch K-Jetronic fuel injection. The idea was partly to make the engine run more smoothly, but mainly to make it easier to meet emissions requirements.

Front radiator

Like with most mid-engined cars, the radiator is mounted in the front where more air can pass through it than in a crowded engine compartment behind the cockpit.

Specifications
1977 Ferrari 308 GTS

ENGINE

Type: V8

Construction: Alloy block and heads

Valve gear: Four inclined valves per cylinder operated by four belt-driven overhead camshafts

Bore and stroke: 3.19 in. x 2.78 in.

Displacement: 2,927 cc

Compression ratio: 9.2:1

Induction system: Four twin-choke Weber carburetors

Maximum power: 205 bhp at 7,000 rpm

Maximum torque: 181 lb-ft at 5,000 rpm

TRANSMISSION

Five-speed manual

BODY/CHASSIS

Square-tube steel chassis with steel two-door, two-seat body with Targa top

SPECIAL FEATURES

The 288 GTO uses the 308's V8 engine mounted longitudinally but with twin turbos and intercoolers.

308s had black bumpers up until the end of production. Later cars had color-coded bumpers.

RUNNING GEAR

Steering: Rack-and-pinion

Front suspension: Double wishbones with coil springs, telescopic shocks and anti-roll bar

Rear suspension: Double wishbones, coil springs, telescopic shocks and anti-roll bar

Brakes: Vented discs, 10.8 in. (front), 11 in. (rear)

Wheels: Alloy, 165 TR390

Tires: Michelin TRX TR390

DIMENSIONS

Length: 172.4 in. **Width:** 67.7 in.

Height: 44 in. **Wheelbase:** 92.1 in.

Track: 57.5 in. (front), 57.5 in. (rear)

Weight: 3,305 lbs.

ITALY 1989–1994

Ferrari **348 TS**

Stricter crash protection regulations and the need for new, up-to-date styling resulted in a bigger, faster replacement for the Ferrari 328. The stunning 348 lasted for only five years before being replaced by the F355.

"...a true thoroughbred."

"Fire up the quad-cam V8 and there's no mistaking that this is a true thoroughbred Ferrari. It's an extraordinary engine, immensely tractable, and yet incredibly punchy at higher engine speeds. It is worth winding the windows down in tunnels just to listen to the howling cams induction and bellowing exhaust. Handling is razor sharp, as you would expect, but the 348 is a twitchy car at the limit, a flaw Ferrari readdressed in the F355."

Supportive seats and analog gauges make the interior of the 348 extremely functional.

Milestones

1973 Ferrari introduces its first mid-engined V8 car, the 308 GT4.

1975 A two-seater version, the sleek 308 GTB, is launched.

The Ferrari 328 bowed out in 1989 in order to make way for the new 3.4-liter 348.

1985 The 3.2-liter 328 replaces the aging 308.

1989 Ferrari launches its replacement for the 328. The new 348 uses a 3.4-liter version of the familiar V8 engine, now mounted longitudinally rather than transversely.

The 348's replacement, the F355, is still being produced.

1994 The amazing F355 is launched and replaces the 348 after five years of production.

UNDER THE SKIN

Twisted motor

The biggest difference between the 328 and the 348 is that the later car has its engine mounted longitudinally rather than transversely. However, the five-speed transmission is mounted transversely. The steel monocoque carries double-wishbone suspension all around, with coil springs and telescopic shock absorbers at each corner and front and rear anti-roll bars. It stops on a dime with change to spare thanks to four-wheel vented discs.

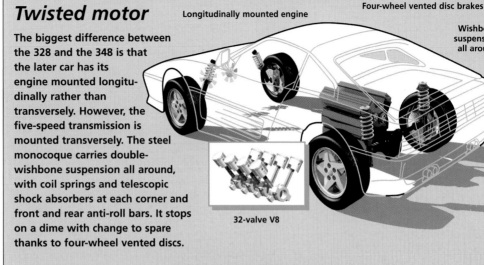

Longitudinally mounted engine

Four-wheel vented disc brakes

Wishbone suspension all around

32-valve V8

THE POWER PACK

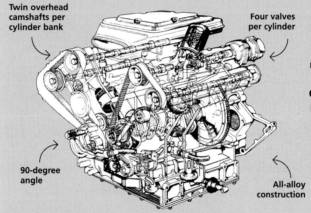

Twin overhead camshafts per cylinder bank

Four valves per cylinder

90-degree angle

All-alloy construction

Thoroughbred V8

The Ferrari 348 gets its name from the engine size. It's a 3.4 liter V8—hence the name 348. The engine can trace it roots back to 1982, when Ferrari fitted new four-valve heads on the 308 Quattro-valvole. It was enlarged to 3.2 liters for the 328 of 1985. In the 348, it is an all-aluminum 90-degree V8 with four valves per cylinder operated by twin overhead camshafts per cylinder bank. Bosch Motronic fuel injection helps the engine produce a healthy 300 bhp at 7,000 rpm and 229 lb-ft of torque at 4,000 rpm.

The name game

When it comes to naming a Ferrari, it couldn't be more elementary. In this case the 348 comes from the 3.4 liter V8 engine. The 'T' signifies that the transmission is mounted transversely instead of longitudinally and the 'S' or 'B' is the body style—S is for Spyder (targa top), B is for Berlinetta (coupe).

The 348 bodies were designed by Pininfarina and built by Scaglietti.

Ferrari **348 TS**

When Ferrari replaced the 328, it did more than just facelift the old car. Substantial reengineering resulted in a true supercar, one of the fastest in the world when it was launched in 1989.

Limited-slip differential

A 40-percent limited-slip differential helps the 348 transfer all its power onto the road with a minimum of fuss.

32-valve V8

The 328's all-alloy V8 was enlarged to 3.4 liters for the 348. However, the 348's engine is mounted longitudinally rather than transversely (first seen on the Ferrari Mondial), and so it can be mounted five inches farther down in the chassis to lower the center of gravity.

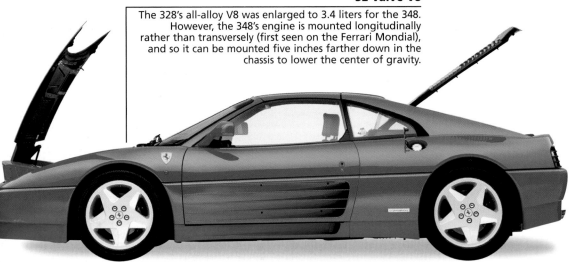

Targa top

While this version is a TS, or targa top, in 1993 Ferrari finally decided to build a full convertible version of its most popular model to date. Ferrari hadn't built a true convertible since the Mondial T Cabriolet in 1989.

Nonfunctional grill

The black front grill is nonfunctional. The engine is cooled with Testarossa-styled side vents located on the the rear section of the doors. Fitting the radiators beside the engine meant that the 348 had to be 5.3 inches wider than its forebear.

Extended wheelbase

Although the 348 is an inch shorter than the 328, its wheelbase is four inches longer. This helps give the 348 greater stability than its predecessor.

Specifications

1993 Ferrari 348 TS

ENGINE

Type: V8

Construction: Alloy block and heads

Valve gear: Four valves per cylinder operated by four overhead camshafts

Bore and stroke: 3.35 in. x 2.95 in.

Displacement: 3,405 cc

Compression ratio: 10.4:1

Induction system: Bosch Motronic M2.5 fuel injection

Maximum power: 300 bhp at 7,000 rpm

Maximum torque: 229 lb-ft at 4,000 rpm

TRANSMISSION

Five-speed manual

BODY/CHASSIS

Unitary monocoque construction with steel two-seater targa body

SPECIAL FEATURES

The 348's rear lights sit behind a stylish, black, slatted cover.

The straked flanks of the 348 are one of its most distinctive styling features.

RUNNING GEAR

Steering: Rack-and-pinion

Front suspension: Double wishbones with coil springs, telescopic shock absorbers and anti-roll bar

Rear suspension: Double wishbones with coil springs, telescopic shock absorbers and anti-roll bar

Brakes: Vented discs (front and rear)

Wheels: Cast-alloy, 7.5 x 17 in. (front), 9 x 17 in. (rear)

Tires: 215/50 ZR17 (front), 255/45 ZR17 (rear)

DIMENSIONS

Length: 166.5 in.　**Width:** 74.6 in.

Height: 46.1 in.　**Wheelbase:** 96.5 in.

Track: 59.1 in. (front), 62.1 in. (rear)

Weight: 3,292 lbs.

Ferrari 360 MODENA

The latest in a great line of midengined Ferraris, the 360 Modena puts its competition to shame. Its incredible Pininfarina-styled bodywork not only looks good but works for a living. It produces an incredible amount of downforce without the need for add-on spoilers.

"...out of this world."

"If you have driven an older midengined Ferrari, you will be surprised when you step into the 360. The interior is much more spacious and user-friendly, but you still know this is a real road racer. On the road the V8 comes on strong at 4,000 rpm, but doesn't run out of steam until 8,500 revs. Combined with the in-street F1 gearshifts, the acceleration feels out of this world. Handling is excellent, but turn off the traction control at your own risk."

Ferrari has taken great pains to make the 360 more comfortable than previous cars.

Milestones

1967 Ferrari launches its
first mid-engined production car. The Dino 206GT uses a 2.0-liter V6. A bigger 2.4-liter engine is fitted to the revised Dino 246GT in 1969.

Ferrari's first midengined production car was the Dino, launched in 1967.

1973 The V6 Dino is replaced
by the new 308 range, using Ferrari's first-ever V8 engine mounted midship. The first model to be launched is the 308GT4, styled by Bertone.

The 360 Modena replaces the older Ferrari F355.

1999 After several other
generations of mid-engined V8 Ferraris, the company launches its latest offering, the 360 Modena. Its 3.6-liter V8 produces an almighty 394 bhp, and its Pininfarina wind-tunnel-crafted body produces unheard of amounts of downforce.

UNDER THE SKIN

Alloy wonder

The 360 is the first Ferrari to use all-aluminum construction. Its spaceframe/monocoque means it is 134 pounds lighter than its predecessor, the F355, despite an increase in overall size. Aluminum double wishbone suspension is used in conjunction with coil springs, anti-roll bars, and adaptive shock absorbers, which react to conditions to give the best possible damping in any given situation. Huge vented disc brakes ensure the 360 stops.

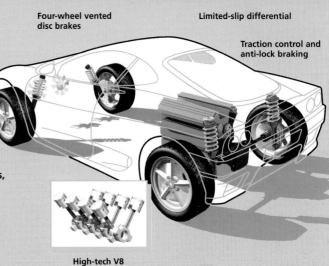

Four-wheel vented disc brakes

Limited-slip differential

Traction control and anti-lock braking

High-tech V8

THE POWER PACK

High-revving V8

The V8 engine powering the 360 is a completely redesigned unit. Displacing 3.6 liters, it has five valves per cylinder (three intake and two exhaust) like the old F355 unit. The valves are actuated by two overhead camshafts per cylinder bank with hydraulic tappets. The block, oil pan and cylinder heads are all cast in light alloy to keep the weight down. Connecting rods are made of titanium, and the pistons are made of forged aluminum. This engine has one of the world's highest specific power outputs at 111 bhp per liter. It produces its maximum power of 394 bhp at a dizzy 8,500 rpm.

Downforce

Despite its lack of big wings or spoilers, the 360 Modena produces more downforce at 70 mph than the F355 could at its top speed. It took thousands of hours in the wind tunnel for Pininfarina to produce this beautiful, yet very functional, design.

Wind tunnel testing shows the 360 to have a drag coefficient of 0.34.

Ferrari 360 MODENA

With the arrival of the latest Porsche 911, Ferrari was forced to raise its game. With the stunning new 360 Modena, the company has done just that. Fantastic looks and technology to match put it at the top of the supercar league.

3.6-liter V8 engine

The 40-valve V8 engine displaces only 3.6 liters yet produces an enormous 394 bhp—that's 111 bhp per liter.

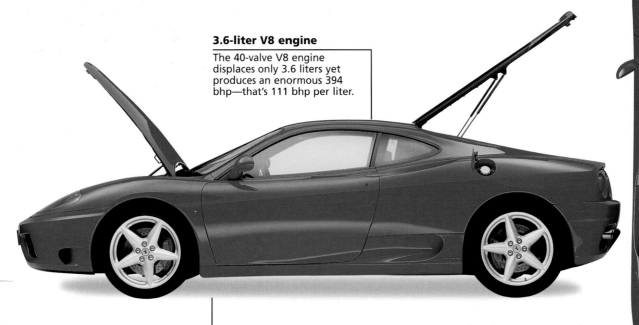

Aluminum suspension

Aluminum is used for the double-wishbone suspension that is fitted in all four corners. Coil springs and adaptive shock absorbers are also featured.

Aluminum construction

The 360 is the first Ferrari to use all-aluminum construction. It is therefore lighter than the F355 despite an increase in size. It is also stiffer.

Fixed headlamps

Pop-up headlights were not used,
as they affect aerodynamics
when raised at high speeds.

Advanced aerodynamics

The 360 is cleverly designed to give
downforce without spoilers or wings.
Even the underbody has been
designed in the wind tunnel.

Specifications

1999 Ferrari 360 Modena

ENGINE

Type: V8

Construction: Alloy block and heads

Valve gear: Five valves per cylinder operated by two overhead camshafts per cylinder bank

Bore and stroke: 3.40 in. x 3.16 in.

Displacement: 3,586 cc

Compression ratio: 11.0:1

Induction system: Bosch multipoint fuel injection

Maximum power: 394 bhp at 8,500 rpm

Maximum torque: 275 lb-ft at 4,750 rpm

TRANSMISSION

Six-speed semi-automatic

BODY/CHASSIS

Aluminum spaceframe/monocoque

SPECIAL FEATURES

Despite all-new styling, the traditional round rear lights are retained.

Once again, Pininfarina has penned stunning lines for a Ferrari.

RUNNING GEAR

Steering: Rack-and-pinion

Front suspension: Double wishbones with coil springs, adaptive shock absorbers and anti-roll bar

Rear suspension: Double wishbones with coil springs, adaptive shock absorbers and anti-roll bar

Brakes: Vented discs (front and rear)

Wheels: Alloy, 18-in. dia.

Tires: 215/45 ZR18 (front), 275/40 ZR18 (rear)

DIMENSIONS

Length: 176.3 in.   **Width:** 75.7 in.

Height: 47.8 in.   **Wheelbase:** 102.4 in.

Track: 65.7 in. (front), 63.7 in. (rear)

Weight: 3,065 lbs.

Ferrari **456 GT**

Occasionally a car appears that has everything: speed, looks, handling, a famous designer, and a famous name. The Ferrari 456 GT is such a car—the world's finest four-seat Grand Tourer.

"...incredibly nimble."

"Need outright speed? Just floor the throttle and there's instant response. The clutch, steering and brakes are light, and the gearshift is easy in its metal gate despite the transmission being mounted at the rear. For a relatively heavy car the 456 GT is incredibly nimble due to its equal weight distribution and high-geared steering. Alternate suspension settings give greater body control and as soft of a ride as desired."

The 456 boasts a well-equipped cabin, with the accent more on luxury than performance.

Milestones

1973 After 1,400 have been sold, the Ferrari Daytona goes out of production. Ferrari turns away from the classic recipe of a V12 engine at the front in favor of a mid-engined layout.

Last of the classic front-engined Ferraris was the 1973 Daytona.

1988 Before Enzo Ferrari dies this year he sees work progress on the 456 GT project, the first front-engined Ferrari since 1973.

The previous four-seater Ferrari was the mid-engined Mondial.

1992 Ferrari launches the 456 GT at the Paris Motor Show.

1996 Supplementing the six-speed transmission version, Ferrari introduces the GTA with its four-speed automatic.

UNDER THE SKIN

Old and new

With the big V12 engine and rear drive, the 456 GT may sound old fashioned however, because the six-speed ZF transmission is mounted at the back with the final drive and limited-slip differential, it has a near equal (52/48) weight distribution. The suspension is classic Ferrari, with double wishbones all around, but it includes electronically adjusting shocks as well as rear self levelling.

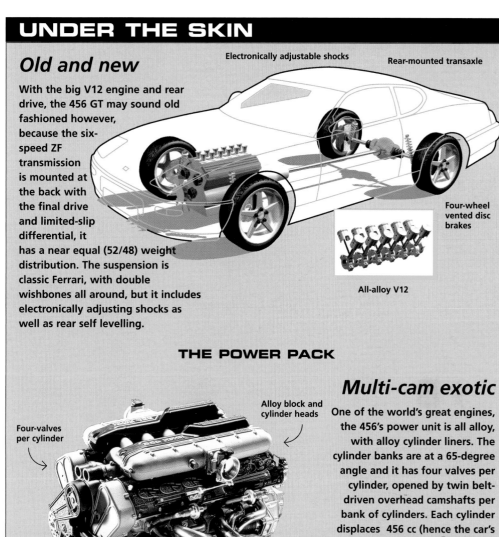

Electronically adjustable shocks

Rear-mounted transaxle

Four-wheel vented disc brakes

All-alloy V12

THE POWER PACK

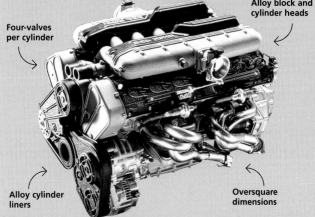

Four-valves per cylinder

Alloy block and cylinder heads

Alloy cylinder liners

Oversquare dimensions

Multi-cam exotic

One of the world's great engines, the 456's power unit is all alloy, with alloy cylinder liners. The cylinder banks are at a 65-degree angle and it has four valves per cylinder, opened by twin belt-driven overhead camshafts per bank of cylinders. Each cylinder displaces 456 cc (hence the car's name) to give its 5.4-liter displacement. It's oversquare, with a bigger bore than stroke to allow it to reach a high rpm.

Shiftless 456

If you can live without the wonderful six-speed transmission or have to drive your 456 in heavy traffic every day, there's the 456 GTA with its electronically controlled four-speed automatic transmission. The performance penalty is tiny.

The 456 is the first front-engined Ferrari since the 365 Daytona.

Ferrari **456 GT**

The 456 GT's smooth styling resembles the Daytona, but it's less macho and more sophisticated for the 1990s. It is one of those rare beautiful cars which goes even faster than it looks.

Automatic windows

The door glass automatically lowers slightly when the door is shut to make closing the door easier. It then returns to its closed position.

V12 engine

Ferrari's all-alloy V12 has a dry sump oil pan for two reasons. It helps keep the height of the engine down to allow for the low hood and it ensures that even during the hardest cornering there is no danger of oil surging away from the oil pump.

Larger rear wheels

Different size wheels and tires front to rear are the norm on high-performance cars. The 456 GT is no exception, with 10-inch wide rear wheels compared with 8-inch wide fronts.

Alloy bodywork

Alloy bodywork has been a Ferrari theme since the earliest days and it's carried on in the 456. The alloy panels are welded to the steel chassis frame to give a rigid overall structure.

Adjustable shocks

The Bilstein shocks adjust automatically to the speed and conditions but the driver can override the automatic system and choose one of three settings; hard, medium or soft according to mood and intentions.

ABS brakes

Ferraris are rarely light. The 456 is a powerful heavyweight with outstanding ABS brakes, using the latest ATE Mk IV system, are standard. The brake calipers are alloy to reduce unsprung weight.

Six-speed transmission

Although the V12 has lots of power and torque, it can be fitted to a six-speed transmission to maximize the acceleration potential and give a relaxed (25.3 mph per 1,000 rpm) top gear for highway cruising.

Specifications

1998 Ferrari 456 GTA

ENGINE

Type: V12

Construction: Alloy block and heads

Valve gear: Four valves per cylinder operated by two belt-driven overhead cams

Bore and stroke: 3.46 in. x 2.95 in.

Displacement: 5,474 cc

Compression ratio: 10.6:1

Induction system: Bosch Motronic M2.7 electronic fuel injection

Maximum power: 435 bhp at 6,250 rpm

Maximum torque: 406 lb-ft at 4,500 rpm

TRANSMISSION

Rear mounted four-speed automatic

BODY/CHASSIS

Tubular steel chassis with two-door 2+2 alloy bodywork

SPECIAL FEATURES

The Ferrari V12 performs as good as its looks suggest.

The 456 GTA is the only Ferrari to be offered with a fully-automatic, four-speed transmission.

RUNNING GEAR

Steering: Rack-and-pinion

Front suspension: Double wishbones with adjustable Bilstein shocks, coil springs and anti-roll bar

Rear suspension: Double wishbones with adjustable Bilstein shocks, coil springs and anti-roll bar

Brakes: Vented discs brakes (front and rear)

Wheels: Alloy, 8 x 17 in. (front), 10 x 17 in. (rear)

Tires: 255/45 ZR17 (front), 285/45 ZR17 (rear)

DIMENSIONS

Length: 186.2 in.   **Width:** 75.6 in.

Height: 51.2 in.   **Wheelbase:** 102.4 in.

Track: 62.4 in. (front), 63.2 in. (rear)

Weight: 4,013 lbs.

Ferrari 550 MARANELLO

It is fitting that Ferrari should choose the name of its home town for its first new front-engined two-seater supercar since 1968. It is the fastest Ferrari currently available, yet is also one of the most practical ever built.

"...blistering performance."

"You are unlikely to come away dissatisfied after driving the 550. As well as blistering performance and a magnificently responsive V12 engine, the Maranello has a sensational chassis that is fluid and minutely adjustable at the throttle. Add in great Brembo brakes, and smooth-shifting six-speed transmission and you have an awesome sports car. It also has lightning fast steering that enables you to negotiate sharp corners with complete confidence."

There are few places that a driver would rather be than behind the wheel of this car.

Milestones

1992 Ferrari launches

the 456 GT, the first of a new breed of front-engined V12 supercars. The new car replaces the ageing, mid-engined 512 TR, itself little more than just a Testarossa with a facelift.

Ferrari's previous flagship model was the Testarossa, which was later known as the 512 TR.

1996 Ferrari invites Michael Schumacher

to its famous Fiorano test track to launch the 550 Maranello and impress the motoring media with his driving skill at the wheel.

The Ferrari 456 GT was the first series production Ferrari with the new V12 engine.

1997 Carrozzeria Scaglietti is a buyers'

plan that allows the owners to personalize their 550 Maranellos by choosing from a large list of trim, luxury, and performance enhancements.

UNDER THE SKIN

State-of-the-art

Underneath the Pininfarina-styled body, the 550's ancestry closely follows the Ferrari 456 GT. It shares the same basic chassis layout, V12 engine, and suspension, which means double wishbones all around, coil springs, anti-roll bars and adjustable shocks. To improve weight distribution, the transaxle is mounted at the rear in front of the differential.

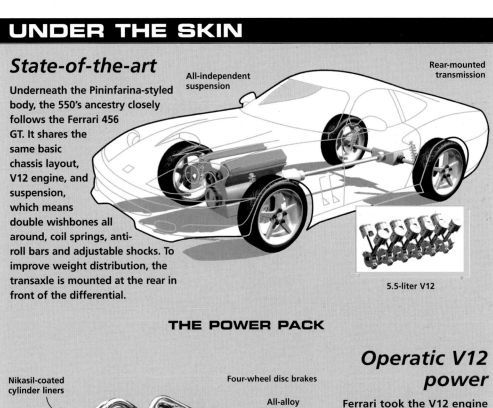

All-independent suspension

Rear-mounted transmission

5.5-liter V12

THE POWER PACK

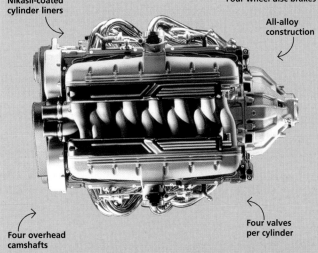

Nikasil-coated cylinder liners

Four-wheel disc brakes

All-alloy construction

Four overhead camshafts

Four valves per cylinder

Operatic V12 power

Ferrari took the V12 engine from the 456 GT and engineered an extra 49 bhp of power. The unit features all-aluminum construction, four overhead camshafts, four valves per cylinder, and variable-geometry inlet and exhaust systems. Equally impressive, this phenomenally powerful engine meets all worldwide emissions requirements. The only disappointment is the sound, which has been muted by noise pollution regulations.

Options list

There is only one 550 model, but the standard specification is impressively complete. An options list is available which allows you to personalize your car. Items include a handling package, carbon-fiber trim, modular wheel rims and tailored luggage.

The 550 is the fastest Ferrari currently available.

Ferrari 550 MARANELLO

Replacing the mid-engined 512M, the new Ferrari 550's appeal is much more broad. The only disappointment is the styling, which critics say fails to meet Pininfarina's highest standard.

Unique wheels and tires

The five-spoke wheels were designed by Pininfarina specifically for the 550. The tires were also specially developed for this model.

V12 power

The 5.5-liter all-alloy V12 engine has a remarkable torque curve, delivering more than 369 lb-ft of torque between 3,600 and 7,000 rpm.

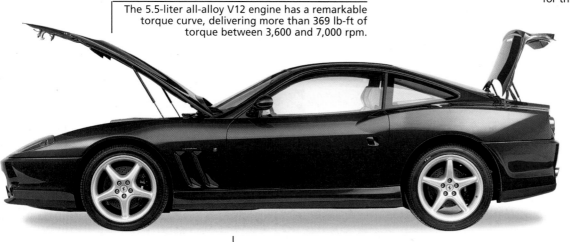

Pininfarina styling

The famous Italian design house Pininfarina was asked to produce a shape which would be a spiritual successor to the great Daytona of the 1970s.

Spacious practicality

Practicality played as large a part in the Maranello's development process as optimum performance. Hence, the car is easy to get into and it has a 6.5 cubic foot capacity trunk.

ASR traction control

Traction control stops the rear wheels from spinning under acceleration. But it is possible to turn it off.

Luxurious interior

The occupants have unrivaled levels of comfort. Standard equipment in the Maranello includes eight-way electrically-adjustable seats, Jaeger LCD analogue instrumentation, air-conditioning, leather upholstery, and a Sony multi-CD player/radio.

Strong aluminum bodywork

The light aluminum body is welded to a steel frame using a special material called Feran. The frame boasts tremendous torsional rigidity of 207 lb-ft/degrees.

Specifications
1998 Ferrari 550 Maranello

ENGINE
Type: V12

Construction: Alloy cylinder block and heads

Valve gear: Four valves per cylinder operated by four overhead camshafts

Bore and stroke: 3.46 in. x 2.95 in.

Displacement: 5,474 cc

Compression ratio: 10.8:1

Induction system: Bosch 5.2 Motronic fuel injection

Maximum power: 485 bhp at 7,000 rpm

Maximum torque: 398 lb-ft at 5,000 rpm

TRANSMISSION
Six-speed manual

BODY/CHASSIS
Steel frame with two-door aluminum coupe body

SPECIAL FEATURES

Cooling vents behind the front wheel arches hark back to the 275 GTB.

It may be a brand-new car, but some things never change on a Ferrari. The 550 Maranello has a traditional alloy shifter gate.

RUNNING GEAR
Steering: Power-assisted rack-and-pinion

Front suspension: Double wishbones with coil springs, telescopic shocks and anti-roll bar

Rear suspension: Double wishbones with coil springs, telescopic shocks and anti-roll bar

Brakes: Vented discs (front and rear)

Wheels: Alloy, 18-in. dia.

Tires: Specially-designed 255/40 ZR18 (front), 295/35 ZR18 (rear)

DIMENSIONS
Length: 179.1 in. **Width:** 76.2 in.

Height: 50.3 in. **Wheelbase:** 98.4 in.

Track: 64.3 in. (front), 62.4 in. (rear)

Weight: 3,726 lbs.

Ferrari **F40**

The F40 did exactly what Ferrari demanded of it—restore its reputation as a builder of the world's most desirable sports cars. The cars had been getting heavier and less hard-edged. The F40 changed all of that.

"…mind-numbing acceleration!"

"Squeeze yourself into the F40's cockpit—there's no doubt that you are in the ultimate road racer. The heavy clutch bites sweetly and the steering is light, even at a crawl. Designed for triple-digit cornering speeds, the stiff suspension gives a jarring ride over urban roads. But flex your foot on the throttle and there's a blur of mind-numbing acceleration. The power is truly explosive, arriving with a ferocity that no other road car can match. Serious recalibration of your senses is needed to adjust to this Ferrari's outrageous performance."

Despite the stripped-down interior, the F40 still has the classic Ferrari alloy gate for the shifter.

Milestones

1947 The first Ferrari

is built by Enzo Ferrari. His philosophy is to build cars which he races as an advertisement for the production models, which benefit from experience gained on the track. This begins Ferrari's road-racing tradition.

250 SWB Berlinetta racing in 1961.

The years between...

Enzo once said that he made cars for young men that only old men could afford. Sadly, the Ferraris that are the most desirable are those competition cars like the GTO, the 250 SWB, and the 288 GTO—cars that ride hard, are noisy and have as few passenger car qualities as possible.

1987 Ferrari's 40th

anniversary is celebrated by the appearance of the F40, the latest in the line. Sliding plastic windows are standard to save weight and the trunk has room for a spare wheel or luggage, but not both.

1992 Production

ends after an estimated 1,315 F40s are produced by the Maranello factory.

UNDER THE SKIN

... strength with amazing lightness

The chassis consists of a tubular steel space-frame to which the engine and other mechanical components are attached. This is stiffened with bonded composite panels made of woven carbon fiber and Kevlar, or Nomex, and glued into place, achieving strength with amazing lightness. Each door weighs less than 3.5 lbs.

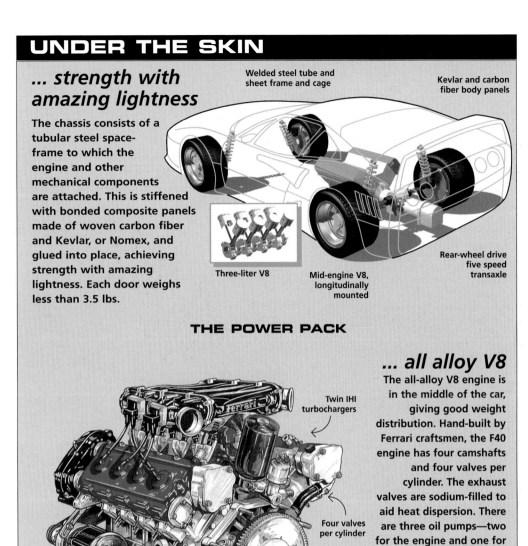

Welded steel tube and sheet frame and cage

Kevlar and carbon fiber body panels

Three-liter V8

Mid-engine V8, longitudinally mounted

Rear-wheel drive five speed transaxle

THE POWER PACK

... all alloy V8

The all-alloy V8 engine is in the middle of the car, giving good weight distribution. Hand-built by Ferrari craftsmen, the F40 engine has four camshafts and four valves per cylinder. The exhaust valves are sodium-filled to aid heat dispersion. There are three oil pumps—two for the engine and one for the transaxle. Each engine was bench tested before it was installed in the car.

Twin IHI turbochargers

Four valves per cylinder

Two overhead camshafts per bank

Silumin alloy block and heads

Racing version

Ferrari developed a racing version of the F40, the F40 LM (for 'Le Mans'). This upgraded and more powerful car debuted in the IMSA series at Laguna Seca in October 1990, finishing a respectable third with Jean Alesi behind the wheel.

Ferrari F40 LM: Power was upped to 630 bhp from the road car's 478 bhp.

Ferrari **F40**

The F40 was designed to be the fastest car that could be driven on European roads. It was the most exciting street-legal Ferrari in 20 years—so exciting that none could be brought to the U.S. for use on the road.

Ground effect

The F40 has a flat bottom, carefully shaped nose and strategically placed air intakes that lead to zero lift in front and downforce at the rear.

Modular wheels

Modular wheels are all light alloy, bolted together with nuts on the inside. Pirelli P-Zero ZR-rated tires were designed for the F40.

Adjustable suspension

Rear suspension has easily adjustable camber (tilting the top of the wheel inward or outward) to tailor handling to suit the driving conditions.

Dual turbos

Dual turbos use exhaust gas to drive them. The compressed air feeds through an intercooler before it enters the engine— the denser the air, the higher the power.

Rear wing

Rear downforce is created by the inverted aerofoil section rear wing.

Three-liter twin-turbo V8

Double overhead cams for each bank of cylinders are driven by a toothed belt. The cylinder heads have two intake and two exhaust valves per cylinder.

Shock absorbers

Front and rear shock absorbers lower height at about 50 mph, improving aerodynamics and handling.

Triple exhaust pipes

Three exhaust pipes exit in the center: one for each bank of cylinders, one for the turbo wastegates.

Cockpit

Brakes and steering have no power boost so that the driver can feel the controls better. There is a choice of three seat sizes.

Dual fuel tanks

Dual fuel tanks have quick-fill caps, 30-gallon capacity. Fuel is fed into the engine by Marelli-Weber fuel injection.

Specifications

1992 Ferrari F40

ENGINE

Type: V8, 90°

Construction: Light alloy, heads, block, Nikasil cylinder liners

Bore and stroke: 3.32 in. x 2.74 in.

Displacement: 2,936 cc

Compression ratio: 7.8:1

Induction system: Two IHI turbos, intercoolers, Marelli-Weber fuel injection, two injectors per cylinder

Ignition: distributorless Marelli-Weber

Maximum power: 478 bhp at 7,000 rpm

Maximum torque: 423 lb-ft at 4,000 rpm

TRANSMISSION

Transaxle: Five speeds forward + reverse (non-synchro optional); pump lubricated; limited slip differential

BODY/CHASSIS

Carbon fiber and Kevlar body panels with welded steel tube cage and suspension mounts

SPECIAL FEATURES

The engine cover is louvered to allow the heat generated by the big V8 and twin turbochargers to be dispersed.

If 478 bhp wasn't enough, a factory kit could add an additional 200 bhp.

RUNNING GEAR

Front suspension: Unequal length wishbones with coil-over shock absorbers, anti-roll bar

Rear suspension: Unequal length wishbones, coil-over shock absorbers, anti-roll bar

Brakes: Vented discs, multi-piston calipers front and rear, separate handbrake caliper

Wheels: Modular light alloy 17 in.

DIMENSIONS

Length: 171.5 in.

Width: 77.5 in.

Height: 44.5 in.

Wheelbase: 96.5 in.

Track: 62.7 in. (front), 63.2 in. (rear)

Weight: 2,425 lbs.

Ferrari **F50**

Ferrari decided to celebrate 50 years of racing and road cars by building the nearest thing possible to a Formula 1 racing car for the road. The result was the incredible F50.

"...the supercar of supercars."

"Formula 1 cars are almost unmanageable for ordinary drivers, but the F50, the supercar of supercars, is very user-friendly. The clutch is hard but progressive, and so you don't immediately stall. The gear shift is very quick and precise. The handling is not in the least twitchy. The F50 is biased to the slightest of understeer, grips the road with force and has a decent ride, but most of all you'll remember the incredible acceleration accompanied by a Grand Prix soundtrack."

The F50's interior is stylish and functional but also extremely basic to keep its weight down.

Milestones

1987 The Ferrari F40 appears
as a celebration of the 40th anniversary of the first Ferrari road car—the 166 Inter with its tiny 1.5-liter V12 engine.

The 288 GTO preceded the F40 and was a homologation special.

1990 Plans are laid for the F50
and Ferrari starts looking at the then-current Formula 1 engine, used to power the cars of Alan Prost and Nigel Mansell, to assess whether it can be adapted as a road car engine.

The F40 was built to celebrate 40 years of Ferraris.

1997 The F50 is built to celebrate
50 years of producing racing and road cars. The racing link explains why Ferrari has built a car with the Formula 1-derived V12 engine and carbonfiber construction. Ferrari intends to make a limited number to make the F50 truly exclusive.

UNDER THE SKIN

Racing derived

It is as advanced as a Formula 1 car for the road should be, with the mid engine mounted rigidly to a carbonfiber monocoque and working through a six-speed transmission with its own heat exchanger. Suspension is by racing-type double wishbones. Pushrods operate the remote mounted shock absorbers and adaptive damping detects the difference between bumps and roll through corners.

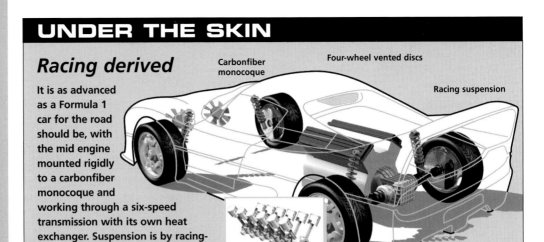

Carbonfiber monocoque

Four-wheel vented discs

Racing suspension

65-degree V12

THE POWER PACK

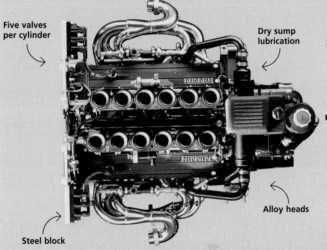

Five valves per cylinder

Dry sump lubrication

Alloy heads

Steel block

Detuned V12

Sometimes referred to as a detuned 1990-era Ferrari F1 engine, there is more to the F50's 65-degree V12 than that. The stroke is lengthened to increase the displacement from the F1's 3.5 liters to 4.7 liters, and this unit revs to only 8,700 rpm rather than 14,000 rpm. Otherwise, it has a cast-iron block with dry-sump lubrication and titanium connecting rods and, of course, four chain-driven camshafts operating 60 valves in total—three intake and two exhaust, per cylinder.

Sleek and fast

The F50 was designed to be driven roofless, even though there is a hardtop. To produce the world's fastest roadster, Ferrari had to make sure that the aerodynamics around the cockpit were right so that wind did not buffet the driver even at high speed.

The F50 looks good with or without its hard top.

Ferrari **F50**

An enlarged Formula 1 engine, carbonfiber construction and racing car pushrod suspension produced the most astounding and fastest street-legal Ferrari ever built.

Formula 1 size brakes

The F50's brakes were as good as those from Formula 1 cars before they switched from metal discs to carbonfiber. They are huge vented discs, nearly 14 inches in diameter at the front.

V12 engine

Power was everything with the F1 engine that formed the basis of the F50's unit. Despite making it 1.2 liters larger, the 4.7-liter V12 still produces only 347 lb-ft of torque compared with its power output of 513 bhp.

Manual windows

The F50 does not have power windows, because the electric motors would add unwanted weight and not be in keeping with a stripped-down road racer.

Adaptive suspension

Electronically-controlled Bilstein shock absorbers are fitted. Sensors determine the difference between bumps in the road and roll as the car corners, so the shocks stiffen in corners, almost acting as an anti-roll bar.

Huge downforce

The F50 needs all the downforce it can produce and there is at least 350 lbs. available. This is due to the huge rear wing and the shape of the underbody, which generates a venturi effect that sucks the car onto the road.

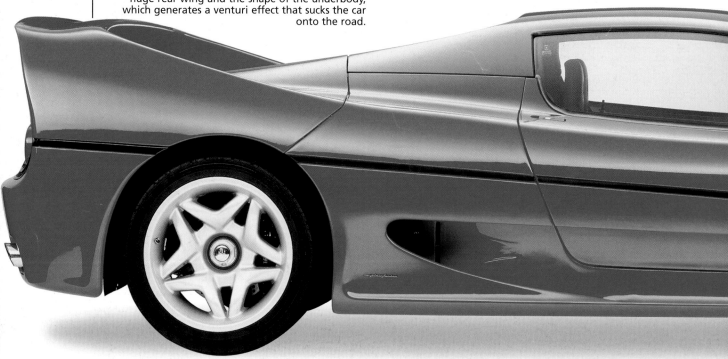

Front cooling vents

Air for the front-mounted radiator is drawn in through the main opening in the nose, and then through the radiator and out of the two huge vents in what would be the hood in an ordinary car.

Rigid-mounted steering

To give the most responsive steering possible, there is no power assistance and the steering rack is mounted rigidly to the body.

Carbonfiber construction

There was never any doubt that the F50 should be made from carbonfiber like an F1 car. Far lighter than steel and also far stronger, it gives the F50 immense torsional rigidity.

Specifications
1997 Ferrari F50

ENGINE

Type: V12

Construction: Steel block and alloy heads

Valve gear: Five valves per cylinder (three inlet, two exhaust) operated by four chain-driven overhead camshafts

Bore and stroke: 3.37 in. x 2.72 in.

Displacement: 4,698 cc

Compression ratio: 11.3:1

Induction system: Bosch Motronic electronic injection

Maximum power: 513 bhp at 8,000 rpm

Maximum torque: 347 lb-ft at 6,500 rpm

TRANSMISSION

Six-speed manual

BODY/CHASSIS

Carbonfiber unitary construction roadster body with separate carbonfiber hardtop

SPECIAL FEATURES

The inboard springs and shock absorbers are actuated with pushrods.

The engine sits under a louvered composite cover.

RUNNING GEAR

Steering: Rack-and-pinion

Front suspension: Double wishbones with inboard pushrod-operated coil springs and shock absorbers with electronic control

Rear suspension: Double wishbones with inboard pushrod-operated coil springs and shock absorbers with electronic control

Brakes: Vented discs, 14-in. dia. (front and rear)

Wheels: Magnesium, 8.5 x 18 in. (front), 13 x 18 in. (rear)

Tires: Goodyear GS-Fiorano, 245/35 ZR18 (front), 335/30 ZR18 (rear)

DIMENSIONS

Length: 176.4 in.   **Width:** 78.2 in.

Height: 44.1 in.   **Wheelbase:** 101.6 in.

Track: 63.8 in. (front), 63.1 in. (rear)

Weight: 3,080 lbs.

Ford **RS200**

Ford's RS200 was planned on paper to be the ultimate Group B World Championship rally car. As it made its debut, however, Group B was abolished, but it remained a supercar on rallycross track and road.

"...a very reassuring package."

"Like every other Group B 'homologation special', the RS200 road car is a compromise. It is quieter and more civilized than the competition car and as fast as the contemporary Ferrari 308 GTB, but not as well equipped. The highly-tuned engine comes into its own on the open road. With the engine kept in the 3,500-6,000 rpm power band, the supple suspension and the grip of the four driven wheels provide a very reassuring package."

Road cars have a more civilized interior than the competition versions.

Milestones

1984 Ford launches a new Group B rally competitor, the RS200. RS denotes that this is to be a Rallye Sport project, while '200' confirms that 200 cars will be produced.

Ford's run of rally domination started with the Mk 1 Escort.

1985 The 200th car leaves the production line. The factory RS200 wins its first event—the Lindisfarne Rally.

1986 The RS200 finishes third in its first World Championship rally in February, and wins its first international rally, the Rally of Ardennes in Belgium. Following horrible crashes in Portugal, Group B rallying is banned.

The Escort RS1800 used a normally-aspirated version of the Cosworth BD-series engine.

1987 The cars will be sold as road cars or for use in rallycross; all orders are to be taken by the end of 1988.

UNDER THE SKIN

Super strong

The RS200's design revolves around the use of a mid-rear positioned engine which drives forward to a massive transmission/differential/front axle assembly, and then to the all-wheel drive. There is also a built-in roll-cage and large tubular subframes which tie the suspension to the tub and the tub to the roll-cage/center section.

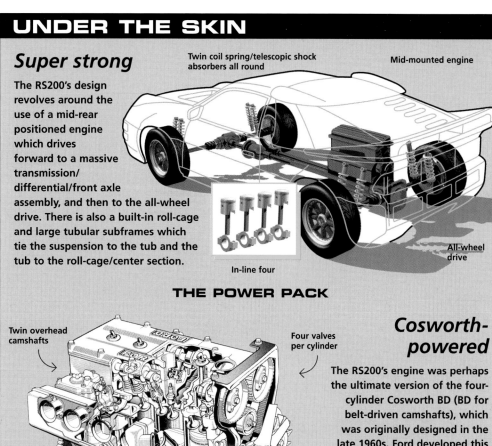

Twin coil spring/telescopic shock absorbers all round

Mid-mounted engine

All-wheel drive

In-line four

THE POWER PACK

Twin overhead camshafts

Four valves per cylinder

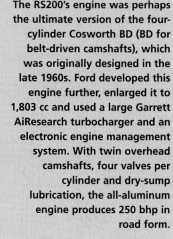

Dry-sump lubrication

All-aluminum construction

Cosworth-powered

The RS200's engine was perhaps the ultimate version of the four-cylinder Cosworth BD (BD for belt-driven camshafts), which was originally designed in the late 1960s. Ford developed this engine further, enlarged it to 1,803 cc and used a large Garrett AiResearch turbocharger and an electronic engine management system. With twin overhead camshafts, four valves per cylinder and dry-sump lubrication, the all-aluminum engine produces 250 bhp in road form.

All white

All RS200s were painted white, and were initially built with figure-hugging Sparco competition seats. Roadgoing cars produced 250 bhp, but up to 700 bhp was available in competition form. Most cars have been used in competition at some stage.

The RS200 makes a fine performance car on road and track.

Ford **RS200**

The RS200 was designed to be the ultimate rally car, to compete in the most challenging arena of international rallying—the terrifying and short-lived Group B championship.

Selectable two-wheel drive

Some of the RS200's rivals featured permanent all-wheel drive, but the RS driver has the option of selecting just rear-wheel drive if desired.

BDT twin-cam

The RS200 is powered by the final development of the Ford BDT (belt-driven turbo) four-cylinder, 16-valve twin-cam engine.

Roof-mounted intercooler

Wind-tunnel tests showed that the ideal location for the intercooler, which feeds cool, dense air to the turbocharger, is on the roof at the top of the engine cover.

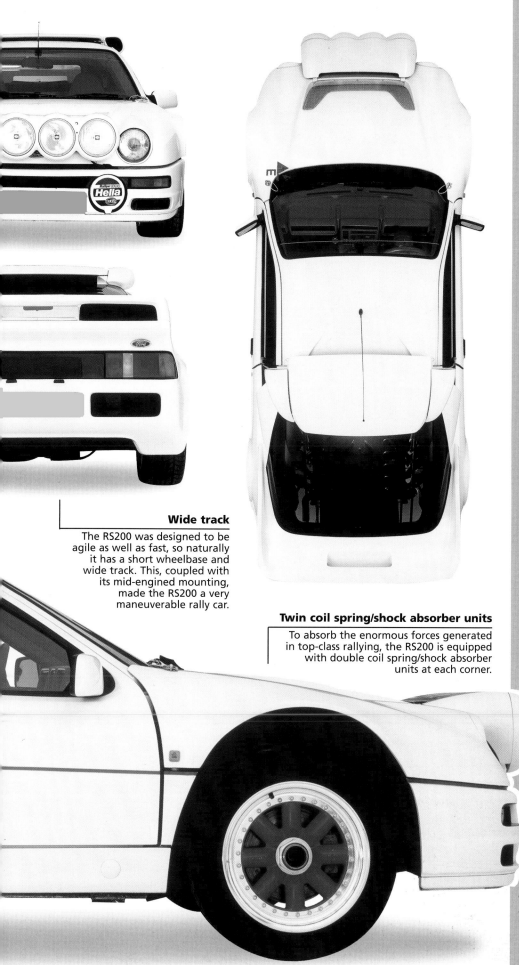

Specifications
1986 Ford RS200

ENGINE
Type: In-line four-cylinder

Construction: Cast-aluminum block and head

Valve gear: Four valves per cylinder operated by twin overhead camshafts

Bore and stroke: 3.38 in. x 3.05 in.

Displacement: 1,803 cc

Compression ratio: 8.2:1

Induction system: Fuel injection with Garrett AiResearch turbocharger

Maximum power: 250 bhp at 6,500 rpm

Maximum torque: 215 lb-ft at 4,000 rpm

TRANSMISSION
Five-speed manual

BODY/CHASSIS
Platform-type chassis with aluminum honeycomb, carbonfiber and steel body

SPECIAL FEATURES

Heavy-duty suspension is used to deal with the rough terrain of a rally stage.

The turbo intercooler is mounted right in the airflow in the rooftop spoiler.

RUNNING GEAR
Steering: Rack-and-pinion

Front suspension: Upper and lower wishbones with double coil spring/telescopic shock absorber units and anti-roll bar

Rear suspension: Upper and lower wishbones with double coil spring/telescopic shock absorber units and anti-roll bar

Brakes: Vented discs, 11.2 in. dia. (front and rear)

Wheels: Aluminum alloy, 8 x 16 in.

Tires: Pirelli P700, 225/50 VR16

DIMENSIONS
Length: 157.5 in.   **Width:** 69.4 in.

Height: 52.0 in.   **Wheelbase:** 99.6 in.

Track: 59.1 in. (front), 59.0 in. (rear)

Weight: 2,607 lbs.

Wide track
The RS200 was designed to be agile as well as fast, so naturally it has a short wheelbase and wide track. This, coupled with its mid-engined mounting, made the RS200 a very maneuverable rally car.

Twin coil spring/shock absorber units
To absorb the enormous forces generated in top-class rallying, the RS200 is equipped with double coil spring/shock absorber units at each corner.

Honda **NSX-R**

The Type-R is the hottest version of the NSX, the stock version of which is sold with Acura badging in the U.S. This performance option is not available on U.S. cars and therefore the Type-R is badged as a Honda and not an Acura.

"...tremendous traction."

"Some of the more civilized auto enthusiasts feel the NSX Type-R is a serious, and hard-core race car because of its incredibly hard suspension settings. Those settings come into their own on smooth roads, where the car hurtles through corners dead flat with the driver held firm in the Recaro seats. Doubling the effect, the limited-slip differential gives tremendous traction. The Honda is still the easiest car in the world to drive at very high speeds with superb handling and plenty of feedback."

Although the Type-R is a lightweight racer, the cabin contains many modern conveniences.

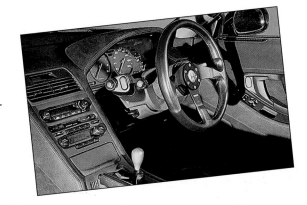

Milestones

1984 Honda starts its ambitious NSX

project. Research includes looking at the world's best supercars to find out how to improve them.

The light Integra Type-R uses techniques honed on the NSX.

1989 The NSX makes its debut at the

Chicago Auto Show in February, over a year before it's due for production.

The NSX is sold with Acura badging only in the U.S.

1990 Production starts at a totally new

factory dedicated to the NSX at the Tochigi Technical Center.

1992 Honda reveals the lightweight NSX Type-R.

This follows a Mugen version with lowered, stiffened suspension and some carbon-fiber bodywork, as well as a 3.2-liter engine.

1997 The 170-mph NSX S.zero is released

using principles of the Type-R.

UNDER THE SKIN

Showcase

The mid-engined NSX is an absolute showcase of advanced technology with more use of aluminum than any other car. The monocoque body/chassis unit is alloy, with three different thicknesses used— 1.2 mm for the outer panels, just 1.0 mm for the roof and 3.0 mm for the inner structural members. Even the suspension arms are alloy to save weight, as are the subframes on which they are mounted. More than 250 lbs. has been saved.

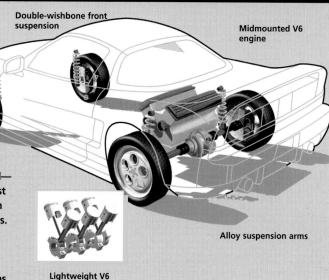

Double-wishbone front suspension

Midmounted V6 engine

Alloy suspension arms

Lightweight V6

THE POWER PACK

Racing expertise

Honda's experience in building some of the world's best racing engines shone through in the original NSX's 274-bhp, 3.0-liter V6. The block and heads are naturally made from alloy and the engine is a compact short-stroke design with four belt-driven overhead camshafts working four valves per cylinder. It benefits from titanium connecting rods that allow the engine to have an 8,000 rpm redline. Not only is there variable valve timing coming into operation around 5,800 rpm, but there is also a variable volume intake system. It operates at the same rpm to give the engine much greater airflow. This raises power to 280 bhp.

Lightweight

Although the regular NSX set the benchmark for supercar handling, the Type-R is more agile with even higher levels of grip and more responsive steering. The trade-off, however, is a very punishing ride on all but the smoothest surface.

The NSX Type-R is a sleek, purposeful performance machine.

Honda **NSX TYPE-R**

Don't be fooled by its looks. The NSX-R retains the beautiful Ferrari-inspired lines of the standard NSX road car, but underneath, there is a blueprinted engine and suspension almost as stiff as a racing car's.

V6 engine
For the Type-R, the 3.0-liter DOHC V6 was fully balanced and blueprinted to withstand competition use. Advertised power and torque remained virtually unchanged at 280 bhp and 209 lb-ft.

Alloy wheels
Not only are the NSX's wheels made from alloy, but they are forged rather than cast to give extra strength. They are also lighter than typical cast-aluminum wheels. The spare tire was deleted to save weight.

VTEC–variable valve timing and lift
By 5,800 rpm, the intake and exhaust valves open farther and longer, thus increasing the engine's power. A hydraulically actuated mechanism locks the cam followers to follow the high lift cam profile.

Weight-saving program
To save 268 lbs., Honda took drastic measures. It scrapped the air conditioning, underseal, stereo, the standard seats and other pieces of electrical equipment.

Wishbone rear suspension

Very wide-based wishbones are used at the rear, and what looks like a steering track rod on each side is in fact an adjustable arm to change the toe angle of the wheels. This gives a measure of passive rear-wheel steer, toeing-in under cornering load.

Alloy body

There was little scope to lighten the body, except for the plastic-covered steel bumpers. For the best compromise between strength and weight, they were changed to alloy.

Specifications

1993 Honda NSX Type-R

ENGINE
Type: V6

Construction: Alloy block and heads

Valve gear: Four valves per cylinder operated by two belt-driven overhead camshafts per bank of cylinders with VTEC-variable valve lift

Bore and stroke: 3.54 in. x 3.07 in.

Displacement: 2,997 cc

Compression ratio: 10.2:1

Induction system: Electronic fuel injection

Maximum power: 280 bhp at 7,300 rpm

Maximum torque: 209 lb-ft at 5,400 rpm

TRANSMISSION
Five-speed manual

BODY/CHASSIS
Aluminum-alloy monocoque with alloy two-door coupe body

SPECIAL FEATURES

The rear window lifts up to give better access to the NSX's midmounted engine.

The alloy wheels are unique to the NSX Type-R and are ultra-lightweight.

RUNNING GEAR
Steering: Rack-and-pinion

Front suspension: Double wishbones with coil springs, telescopic shock absorbers and anti-roll bar

Rear suspension: Double wishbones with coil springs, telescopic shock absorbers and anti-roll bar

Brakes: Vented discs, 11.1-in. dia.

Wheels: Alloy 6.5 x 15 in. (front), 8.0 x 16 in. (rear)

Tires: 205/50 ZR15 (front), 225/50 ZR16 (rear)

DIMENSIONS
Length: 173.4 in.   **Width:** 71.3 in.

Height: 46.1 in.   **Wheelbase:** 99.6 in.

Track: 59.4 in. (front), 60.2 in. (rear)

Weight: 2,712 lbs.

Iso **GRIFO**

This car was conceived by Renzo Rivolta as a rival to Ferraris and Lamborghinis. But beneath the Grifo's elegant Italian lines beats the heart of an all-American Chevrolet Corvette V8.

"...seriously underrated."

"The Grifo is probably the best marriage of Italian engineering and style with the power and durability of a Detroit powerplant. The Corvette V8 may lack the pure-bred feel of an Italian V12, but it produces the necessary horsepower. To match its raw power, the Grifo carves corners perfectly, with enough power to limit its tendency to understeer while going through turns. This is a seriously underrated car."

Inside, the Grifo was sumptuously furnished with leather trim. Optional air-conditioning and wood trim contributes to its luxury feel.

Milestones

1963 A stunningly
beautiful A3 Lusso (road car)
and a competition racer (A3/C)
debut at the Turin Motor Show.

**1965 The Grifo,
with** its exotic Italian styling
and American V8 power, enters
production. A racing variant
makes its debut at Sebring in
1964, but fails to make its mark.

*The Iso A3/C competition racer
ran in 1964 and 1965.*

1968 Iso introduces
a second Grifo. Called the 7-Liter,
this has a longer front end and
raised hood housing a 427-cubic
inch big-block V8. It is capable of
speeds of up to 170 mph.

*The four-seater Iso Lele competed
with Lamborghini's Espada.*

1970 A facelift
introduces a much lower nose
housing semi-retractable
headlights. The standard engine
is a 327 (5.4 liter) V8.

1974 Rising insurance
rates and the oil crisis spell the
demise for the Grifo and
production ends.

UNDER THE SKIN

Clever chassis

The Grifo was effectively constructed by
hand. Stamped steel pressings were
welded to the floorpan for
maximum stiffness.
The independent
front
suspension
used coil
springs and
unequal length
wishbones. The rear
consists of a de Dion axle
with twin radius arms and a
Watt linkage. It also uses Dunlop
four-wheel disc brakes.

Wishbone front
suspension

De Dion rear axle

Welded
monocoque

Small-block V8

THE POWER PACK

American power

Unlike many of its Italian
rivals, instead of an exotic
multi-cam engine, it used a
mass-market cast-iron
American V8. The classic 327-
cubic inch (5.4-liter) small-block
Chevy installed in the Grifo
had forged-steel connecting
rods, a finned alloy oil pan,
hydraulic valve lifters and a
four-barrel carburetor. In 1968
the solid-lifter big-block 427-
cubic inch (7-liter) 'Mark IV'
Chevy engine was
incorporated, resulting in the
Grifo 7-liter (renamed the Can
Am in 1970).

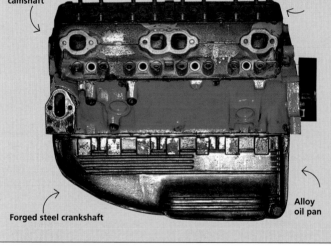

High-lift
camshaft

Large-valve
cylinder
heads

Forged steel crankshaft

Alloy
oil pan

Small changes

During the course of its life cycle, Grifo styling was evolutionary.
The new 1968 7-Liter model introduced a bulged hood and longer
front end. Half-covered headlights were fitted for 1970, updating
the car's looks for the new decade.

*The post-1969 Grifos
boast slightly cleaner
front-end styling.*

Iso **GRIFO**

Iso may not have the heritage of some of its rivals, but for a brief moment in the 1960s, the Italian company produced one of the fastest production supercars in the world.

Luggage space

Although capable of speeds in excess of 150 mph, the Grifo is a true GT, so it has room for a couple of suitcases in the trunk.

Heart of a Corvette

The small-block V8, which was also used in the Corvette, initially displaced 327 cubic inch (5.4 liters) and produced 340 or 350 bhp.

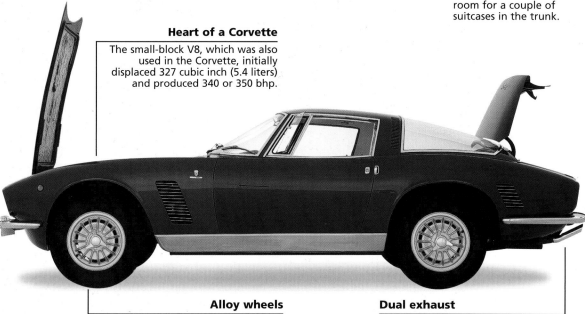

Alloy wheels

Most Grifos are fitted with these handsome cast-alloy wheels, complete with knock-off spinners.

Dual exhaust

To exploit the V8s power, dual exhaust is mandatory and gives a fantastic exhaust note.

Excellent visibility

A large rear window offers great visibility and came with a standard built-in defroster.

Wishbone suspension
The Grifo followed 1960s supercar practice by using unequal length wishbones and coil springs.

Elegant shape
The Grifo was designed by a young Giorgetto Giugiaro, who has been responsible for many of the world's most elegant cars.

Specifications
1967 Iso Grifo

ENGINE
Type: V8
Construction: Cast-iron block and heads
Valve gear: Two valves per cylinder operated by pushrods and rocker arms
Bore and stroke: 4.0 in. x 3.25 in.
Displacement: 5,359 cc
Compression ratio: 10.5:1
Induction system: Single four-barrel Holley carburetor
Maximum power: 350 bhp at 5,800 rpm
Maximum torque: 360 lb-ft at 3,600 rpm

TRANSMISSION
ZF five-speed manual

BODY/CHASSIS
Monocoque two-door coupe

SPECIAL FEATURES

Side scoops on the front fenders are functional and vent hot air from the engine bay.

Bertone was responsible for building the beautiful coupe body.

RUNNING GEAR
Steering: Burman recirculating ball
Front suspension: Upper and lower wishbones with coil springs and telescopic shocks
Rear suspension: De Dion axle with coil springs, telescopic shocks, anti-roll bar, Watt linkage, and radius arms
Brakes: Servo-assisted disc brakes all around
Wheels: Cast-alloy knock-off
Tires: Pirelli Cinturato 205HS/15

DIMENSIONS
Length: 174.7 in.   **Width:** 69.5 in.
Height: 47 in.   **Wheelbase:** 106.3 in.
Track: 55.5 in. (front and rear)
Weight: 3,036 lbs.

Jaguar XJ13

Number 13 turned out to be unlucky for this spectacular Jaguar racing car. Conceived so that Jaguar could relive its Le Mans glories of the 1950s, it never raced but its legacy lived on in the V12-powered Jaguar road cars.

"...unforgettable experience."

"Although the XJ13 is nearly 75 inches wide, half of that width is taken up by the sills and the cockpit is incredibly cramped— the two occupants actually have to overlap shoulders. Fire it up and the sound is unforgettable: ear-splittingly loud, almost violent. The twin-plate clutch is very jerky and the gearshift is awkward, but once out on the circuit all this is forgotten as the XJ13 unleashes its true potential."

The XJ13's driving position might be snug, but it wasn't designed for cruising.

Milestones

1964 Jaguar completes the prototype of its V12 engine project.

1965 Construction of the XJ13 bodyshell begins.

Jaguar's D-type proved highly successful in the late 1950s.

1966 The XJ13 sports racer is completed and in July breaks the British speed record for a closed circuit run at 161.6 mph. However, Jaguar merges with BMC and the XJ13 project is permanently put on hold.

The most recent Jaguar supercar is the limited production XJ220.

1971 During a promotional event Norman Dewis rolls the XJ13 after a wheel collapses and almost destroys it.

1972 New Jaguar chief executive 'Lofty' England discovers the XJ13 under dust sheets and has it restored.

UNDER THE SKIN

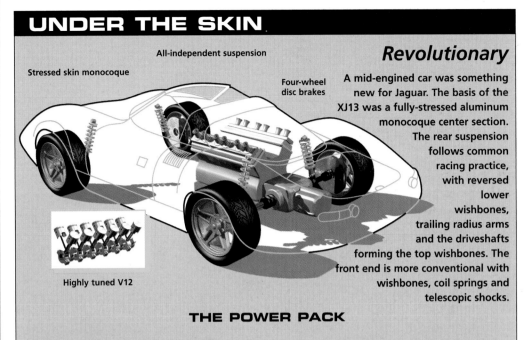

All-independent suspension

Stressed skin monocoque

Four-wheel disc brakes

Highly tuned V12

Revolutionary

A mid-engined car was something new for Jaguar. The basis of the XJ13 was a fully-stressed aluminum monocoque center section. The rear suspension follows common racing practice, with reversed lower wishbones, trailing radius arms and the driveshafts forming the top wishbones. The front end is more conventional with wishbones, coil springs and telescopic shocks.

THE POWER PACK

Monster V12 engine

Many years before Jaguar announced the famous V12 engine which powers the E-Type and XJ sedans, the company developed a very special and quite different V12 for the XJ13. The alloy block had dry liners and boasted a displacement of 5.0 liters, dry sump lubrication and two-stage chain drive to its four camshafts. It is a heavy engine, weighing 639 lbs. Initially, the engine produced 430 bhp at 7,500 rpm, but fine tuning increased power to 502 bhp at 7,600 rpm during one static engine test.

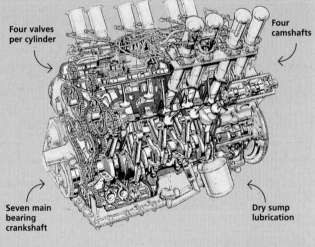

Four valves per cylinder

Four camshafts

Seven main bearing crankshaft

Dry sump lubrication

One and only

The one XJ13 that was built is today jealously guarded by Jaguar. It occasionally appears at classic car shows when Jaguar brings the old beast out of retirement from its museum. However, only a very lucky few are allowed to take the wheel.

Only one original XJ13 was produced, but there are a number of replicas.

Jaguar **XJ13**

Even as Jaguar drew the curtains on its racing program in the 1950s, insiders were planning a spectacular comeback. The XJ13 was the result, but politics and changing regulations caused its demise.

Ultra wide tires

For maximum grip, the XJ13 was fitted with 10-inch front tires and 13.6 rear tires. It was very unusual for a car of the 1960s to have tires this wide.

Stressed engine

Following the lead of the Lotus 25 Formula 1 car, the XJ13's engine is a stressed part of the monocoque structure.

Unique V12 engine

The XJ13 engine is a complex, double overhead camshaft racing unit, while the eventual roadgoing V12 used in the E-Type S3 is a much more practical single overhead camshaft design and is far more reliable.

Six ZF transmissions

Jaguar had six ZF 5DS25/2 transaxles made for the XJ13 because it was easier to change the transmission than just the differential. Each of the six units had a different final drive ratio.

Alloy wheels

The magnesium alloy wheels were cast especially for the XJ13, and featured knock-on spinners. When the car was restored in the mid-1970s, an entirely new set of wheels were fitted as the existing ones were showing signs of fatigue.

Timeless elegance

The XJ13's graceful lines were styled by Malcolm Sayer, the very gifted designer of the great C-Type and D-Type racers of the 1950s. He also penned the immortal E-Type. The overall shape is very aerodynamically efficient, with a low body and minimal frontal area. It is claimed that its drag coefficient is superior to that of the Ford GT40.

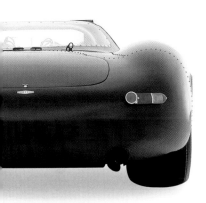

Aluminum monocoque

The key to the XJ13's light weight is its superb monocoque made entirely of aluminum. It is fully stressed and clothed in light alloy bodywork by Abbey Panels of Coventry, England. The engine is mounted directly to the monocoque, and doesn't use rubber bushings.

Specifications
1966 Jaguar XJ13

ENGINE
Type: V12
Construction: Aluminum cylinder block and heads
Valve gear: Two valves per cylinder operated by two chain-driven overhead camshafts per bank
Bore and stroke: 3.42 in. x 2.75 in.
Displacement: 4,991 cc
Compression ratio: 10.4:1
Induction system: Lucas fuel injection
Maximum power: 502 bhp at 7,600 rpm
Maximum torque: 365 lb-ft at 5,500 rpm

TRANSMISSION
Five-speed manual

BODY/CHASSIS
Aluminum monocoque with two-door open-roof coupe body

SPECIAL FEATURES

The intake tubes dominate the view of the engine from the rear.

For maximum grip the one-off Jag uses 15-inch alloys with 10-inch wide tires in the front and 13.6-inch tires on the rear.

RUNNING GEAR
Steering: Rack-and-pinion
Front suspension: Double wishbones with coil springs, shocks and anti-roll bar
Rear suspension: Trailing links with fixed length driveshafts, bottom A-frame with coil springs, shocks and anti-roll bar
Brakes: Vented discs (front and rear)
Wheels: Magnesium alloy, 15-in. dia.
Tires: Dunlop Racing, 4.75/10.00 x 15 (front), 5.30/13.60 x 15 (rear)

DIMENSIONS
Length: 176.4 in.   **Width:** 73 in.
Height: 37.9 in.   **Wheelbase:** 95.9 in.
Track: 55.9 in. (front), 55.9 in. (rear)
Weight: 2,477 lbs.

Jaguar **XJ220**

Hand-made by craftsmen and race-proven at Le Mans, the XJ220 was to be the ultimate sporting Jaguar for the 21st Century. Yet the prototype of this superb machine was built without funding by Jaguar's engineers on their own time.

"...a predator ready to pounce."

"Sit in most supercars and you will find that creature comforts definitely take second place to performance. But the XJ220 is unique, cocooning you in traditional Jaguar luxury. The interior reeks of sumptuous leather. Air conditioning? Of course! Settle back—there's room for the tallest driver. But make no mistake, this cat crouches low like a predator ready to pounce. 100 mph is reached in just 7.3 seconds when you floor the accelerator. The mid-rear engine placement assures beautiful balance and the chassis offers massive structural integrity."

The wrap-around dash houses a complete set of instruments. Despite the car's performance, this is no stripped-down racing car, but a luxury Jaguar.

Milestones

1988 The XJ220 prototype is unveiled to cheers at the British International Auto Show. Designed in secret, it has a 12-cylinder 5,999-cc motor, all-wheel drive and a planned top speed of 200 mph plus. Dozens of potential buyers come forward saying, "We'll have one—at any price."

The XJ220 made full use of Jaguar's endurance racing technology.

1989 Jaguar announces "the XJ220 you can buy" with a 24-valve V6 turbocharged engine, rear-wheel drive—and a planned top speed of more than 220 mph; 350 orders are accepted from 1,000 applications.

1992 In testing at Nardo, Italy an XJ220 achieves 217.3 mph, making it the world's fastest production road car—a tag now assumed by the smaller McLaren F1. Given a long enough straightaway, it should be possible for the XJ220 to reach the magic 220 mph.

1994 The last of the 281 production run of XJ220s come off the line. A price of $706,000 made it impossible to sell every car in a world hit by recession, but those who did take delivery, like rock star Elton John, own the fastest Jaguar ever.

UNDER THE SKIN

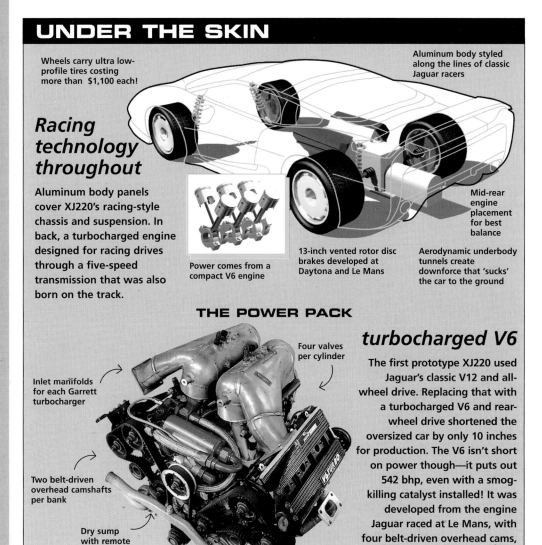

Wheels carry ultra low-profile tires costing more than $1,100 each!

Aluminum body styled along the lines of classic Jaguar racers

Racing technology throughout

Aluminum body panels cover XJ220's racing-style chassis and suspension. In back, a turbocharged engine designed for racing drives through a five-speed transmission that was also born on the track.

Power comes from a compact V6 engine

Mid-rear engine placement for best balance

13-inch vented rotor disc brakes developed at Daytona and Le Mans

Aerodynamic underbody tunnels create downforce that 'sucks' the car to the ground

THE POWER PACK

Inlet manifolds for each Garrett turbocharger

Four valves per cylinder

Two belt-driven overhead camshafts per bank

Dry sump with remote oil tank

turbocharged V6

The first prototype XJ220 used Jaguar's classic V12 and all-wheel drive. Replacing that with a turbocharged V6 and rear-wheel drive shortened the oversized car by only 10 inches for production. The V6 isn't short on power though—it puts out 542 bhp, even with a smog-killing catalyst installed! It was developed from the engine Jaguar raced at Le Mans, with four belt-driven overhead cams, 24 valves and 3.5 liters.

Elegant strength

Although constructed mostly from aluminum, the XJ220 is no lightweight. Its smooth, sensuous lines hide an extremely advanced honeycomb construction. The immensely strong panels and chassis give the car massive structural integrity—after its government crash test, the XJ220's glazing remained intact, and all doors and rear panels opened normally!

Open lids of radiator, engine and tiny luggage compartment.

Jaguar **XJ220**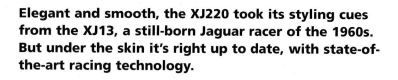

Elegant and smooth, the XJ220 took its styling cues from the XJ13, a still-born Jaguar racer of the 1960s. But under the skin it's right up to date, with state-of-the-art racing technology.

Baggage space
This is a car for traveling light. The rear end is full of engine, and the front is full of radiators to cool it. The trunk is just big enough for a briefcase or two.

Transparent engine cover
The hood on the XJ220 is a lift-up glass panel that puts the powerful turbo motor permanently on show.

Aluminum-honeycomb chassis
Designed to be simple and easy to produce (because the first XJ220 was built in Jaguar engineers' spare time), the chassis is bonded together with adhesive, not welded.

V6 turbo engine
Light and compact, the engine was designed for Jaguar's IMSA race cars in the late-1980s. Adapted for road use, it produces 542 bhp, more than the big V12 originally planned for the car.

Luxury interior
Leather seats, lush carpets and a top-level sound system ensure that XJ220 owners know they're in a Jaguar.

Aluminum body
Lightweight aluminum is used for the body. Each car was hand-assembled before being painted one of five standard colors—all metallics. Cars were available in silver, grey, blue, green and maroon.

King-size wheels and tires

Specially-designed tires and wheels are so big there's no room for a spare. If a tire goes flat, it's filled with a special aerosol mixture and can be driven up to 60 miles at 30 mph.

Aerodynamic styling

Designed to look as elegant as a Jaguar should, the XJ220 is also aerodynamically efficient. At high speeds, the car develops over nearly 600 lbs. of downforce to hold it on the road.

Street legal

The XJ220 is legal for road use in most parts of the world, but not in the U.S. Jaguar never exported any cars to the States, although 10 were sent there for a TV race series in 1993.

Specifications
1993 Jaguar XJ220

ENGINE

Type: V6 turbocharged, 60°
Construction: Aluminum alloy block and heads
Bore and stroke: 3.7 in. x 3.3 in.
Displacement: 3,494 cc
Compression ratio: 8.3:1
Induction system: Electronic injection with twin Garrett turbochargers with air-to-air intercoolers and wastegate control
Maximum power: 542 bhp at 7,200 rpm
Maximum torque: 475 lb-ft at 4,500 rpm

TRANSMISSION

Transaxle: FF Developments all-synchromesh, five-speed manual transaxle with triple-cone synchronizer on first and second gears; Viscous control limited-slip differential

BODY/CHASSIS

Aluminum alloy honeycomb monocoque with alloy two-door, two-seat body

SPECIAL FEATURES

Stylish air outlets for radiator compartment at front.

Vents behind doors feed air to engine's twin intercoolers.

RUNNING GEAR

Front suspension: Independent, double unequal-length wishbones, push-rod and rocker-operated spring/shock units, anti-roll bar
Rear suspension: Independent, unequal-length double wishbones, rocker-operated twin spring/shock units, anti-roll bar
Brakes: Vented 13 in. (front), 11.8 in. (rear), four-piston calipers
Wheels: Die-cast aluminum alloy. 9 in. x 17 in. (front), 10 in. x 18 in. (rear)
Tires: 255/45 ZR17 (front), 345/35 ZR18 (rear)

DIMENSIONS

Length: 194 in.   **Width:** 87.4 in.
Height: 45.3 in.
Wheelbase: 103.9 in.
Track: 67.3 in. (front), 62.5 in. (rear)
Weight: 3,241 lbs.

Jensen INTERCEPTOR

Unveiled in 1966, the Interceptor had everything: Italian styling, American V8 power and well-balanced handling. The original Interceptor remained in production, virtually unaltered, for 10 years and gained a cult following which lives on today.

"...a sense of refinement."

"More of a grand tourer than a sports car, the Interceptor has deep, comfortable seats. The powerful American V8 and automatic transmission are perfectly suited to a laid-back approach to driving and give the car a sense of refinement. Despite its mannerisms, the car is still quick and can reach 60 mph in just over six seconds. Despite its weight, the Jensen has predictable handling, but the brakes are hard pressed to stop the it from speeds above 124 mph."

Full instrumentation is standard and the interior trim is of the highest quality.

Milestones

1966 Jensen presents two vehicles styled by Vingale at the London Motor Show. One is fitted with a specially-developed four-wheel drive system.

Jensen's 1954 541 had triple carburetors and four-wheel disc brakes

1969 An improved Mk II Interceptor is launched. It has a bigger fuel tank, radial tires, and restyled bumpers.

1971 The Mk III and an SP model with three two-barrel carburetors and 330 bhp are introduced. The FF is dropped this year.

1976 Jensen goes out of business and the last original Interceptor is built.

The forerunner of the Interceptor was the bizarre-looking CV8.

1983 A new Mk IV Interceptor enters production, built by Jensen Parts and Service.

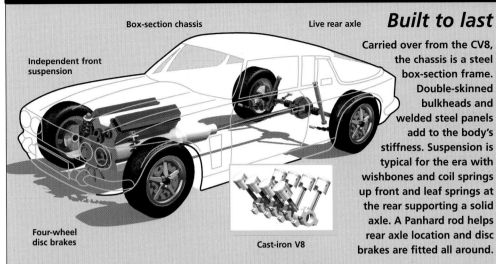

Box-section chassis

Live rear axle

Independent front suspension

Four-wheel disc brakes

Cast-iron V8

Built to last

Carried over from the CV8, the chassis is a steel box-section frame. Double-skinned bulkheads and welded steel panels add to the body's stiffness. Suspension is typical for the era with wishbones and coil springs up front and leaf springs at the rear supporting a solid axle. A Panhard rod helps rear axle location and disc brakes are fitted all around.

THE POWER PACK

Chrysler V8 power

Original Interceptors are powered by Chrysler 383-cubic inch (6.3-liter) and 440-cubic inch (7.2-liter) V8s. Both engines are made of cast-iron with chain-driven camshafts, a five main-bearing crankshaft and two valves per cylinder. With the larger unit acceleration is phenomenal, although handling naturally suffers. Mark IV cars use a small-block 5.9-liter V8, based on the early 340-cubic inch unit. This produced improved fuel economy and slightly better handling.

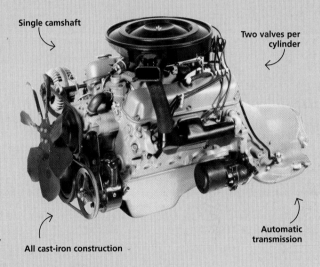

Single camshaft

Two valves per cylinder

All cast-iron construction

Automatic transmission

Hi-tech FF

Standing for Ferguson Formula, the Jensen FF has four-wheel drive, rack-and-pinion steering, and anti-lock brakes. Slightly longer than the standard Interceptor, it is a complex machine and only 320 were built. Only a small number still remain today.

The Jensen FF was in production from 1966 to 1971.

Jensen INTERCEPTOR 🇬🇧

The Jensen Interceptor, launched in 1966 at the London Motor Show, is by far the company's best-remembered product and its biggest seller. The car was so good that it was reborn in the early 1980s.

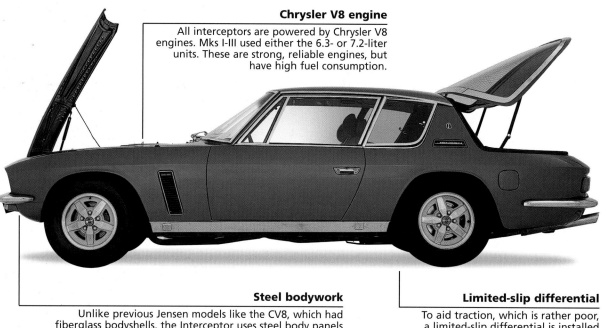

Chrysler V8 engine

All interceptors are powered by Chrysler V8 engines. Mks I-III used either the 6.3- or 7.2-liter units. These are strong, reliable engines, but have high fuel consumption.

Steel bodywork

Unlike previous Jensen models like the CV8, which had fiberglass bodyshells, the Interceptor uses steel body panels which are better suited to high-volume production.

Limited-slip differential

To aid traction, which is rather poor, a limited-slip differential is installed to the rear axle.

Glass hatchback

The bulbous back window is not only attractive, but also functional. The whole unit lifts up to provide space for luggage.

Adjustable shocks

Despite its archaic rear leaf springs, the Interceptor has adjustable telescopic shocks to help smooth out the ride.

Italian styling

The shape was originally penned by Touring of Milan and adapted by Vignale to produce the Interceptor.

Specifications

1968 Jensen Interceptor

ENGINE

Type: V8

Construction: Cast-iron block and heads

Valve gear: Two valves per cylinder operated by hydraulic tappets, pushrods and rockers

Bore and stroke: 4.25 in. x 3.38 in.

Displacement: 6,276 cc

Compression ratio: 10.0:1

Induction system: Single Carter AFB four-barrel carburetor

Maximum power: 330 bhp at 4,600 rpm

Maximum torque: 450 lb-ft at 2,800 rpm

TRANSMISSION

Chrysler TorqueFlite 727 automatic

BODY/CHASSIS

Tubular and welded sheet steel monocoque with two-door body

SPECIAL FEATURES

The Mk II Interceptor has a different front bumper with the parking lights positioned beneath it.

Fender extractor vents aid engine cooling and help to distinguish the Interceptor from the four-wheel drive FF, which has two vents per side.

RUNNING GEAR

Steering: Recirculating ball

Front suspension: Independent wishbones with coil springs and telescopic shocks

Rear suspension: Live rear axle with semi-elliptical leaf springs, telescopic shocks and a Panhard rod

Brakes: Girling discs, 11.4-in. dia. (front), 10.7-in. dia. (rear)

Wheels: Rostyle pressed steel, 15-in. dia.

Tires: Dunlop 185 x 15

DIMENSIONS

Length: 188 in.   **Width:** 70 in.

Height: 53 in.   **Wheelbase:** 105 in.

Track: 56 in. (front and rear)

Weight: 3,696 lbs.

ITALY 1982–1985

Lancia **RALLY 037**

Designed quickly to give Lancia a shot at the World Rally Championship before cars with four-wheel drive dominated the scene, the supercharged, mid-engined Rally 037 was a huge success, winning the title in 1983.

"...a real competition car."

"Sit in the stripped-out interior and close the flimsy doors and you know this is a real competition car. There are no rubber suspension bushings and so the ride is harsh; it's worth it though because it helps give perfectly balanced mid-engined handling. Turn-in is sharp, and there's such huge grip that it's nearly impossible to lose the back of the car on dry pavement. The steering is direct, the clutch is heavy and the ZF transmission needs a firm hand."

There are no creature comforts in the cabin of the Group B 037 rally car.

Milestones

1981 Lancia designs its new
rally car using the center section of the Montecarlo Turbo which is already used for racing. The 037 name comes from Abarth's project number.

The production Montecarlo gave little more than its silhouette to the 037.

1982 The necessary 200 cars
are built to satisfy homologation. The following 20 'Evolution' cars have fuel injection and some Kevlar body panels. The 037's first win comes in the Pace National rally.

Roadgoing Rally 037s are rare and desirable.

1983 Victory in the Monte Carlo
Rally is the first ever win for a supercharged car. The Rally 037 goes on to win the World Rally Championship.

1984 The Evolution 2 version
of the 037 is built. It has a 2,111-cc engine with 325 bhp. Lancia builds 20 of these in 1984 and 1985.

UNDER THE SKIN

Monte midriff

Lancia took the center section of its mid-engined road car—the Beta Montecarlo—and added tubular-steel subframes at each end to carry the longitudinal, mid-mounted engine. It uses a full race rally type suspension. This is very different from the Montecarlo, featuring wide-spaced wishbones and long coil springs with dual shocks at the rear.

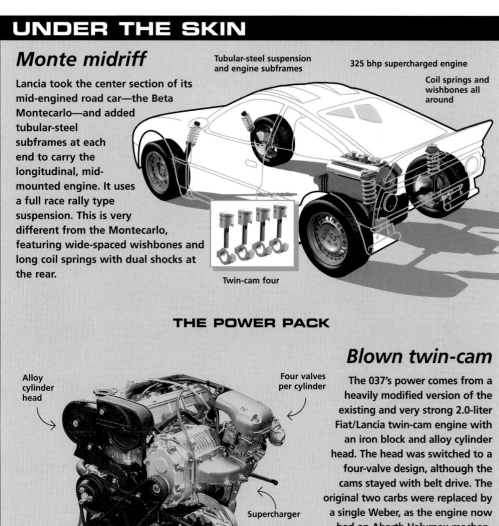

Tubular-steel suspension and engine subframes

325 bhp supercharged engine

Coil springs and wishbones all around

Twin-cam four

THE POWER PACK

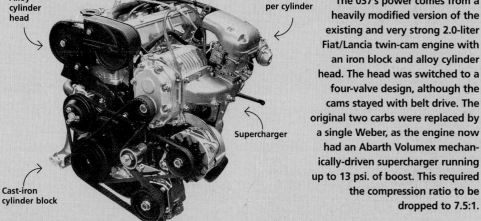

Alloy cylinder head

Four valves per cylinder

Supercharger

Cast-iron cylinder block

Blown twin-cam

The 037's power comes from a heavily modified version of the existing and very strong 2.0-liter Fiat/Lancia twin-cam engine with an iron block and alloy cylinder head. The head was switched to a four-valve design, although the cams stayed with belt drive. The original two carbs were replaced by a single Weber, as the engine now had an Abarth Volumex mechanically-driven supercharger running up to 13 psi. of boost. This required the compression ratio to be dropped to 7.5:1.

Ultimate Evo

The ultimate Rally 037 is the Evolution 2 version, 20 of which were built in 1984 and 1985. They had the engine size increased to 2,111 cc with a larger bore and longer stroke. This helped to increase the power to 325 bhp at 8,000 rpm.

Evolution 2 037s only came in full rally trim—there were no road cars.

Lancia RALLY 037

The Lancia Rally 037 is one of those special breed of cars designed to compete in the exciting Group B rally championship. It is hugely effective and terrifyingly fast.

Huge rear spoiler

The huge rear spoiler had to be homologated, but it was really only necessary on the more powerful competition cars which needed to maximize their traction.

Twin-cam engine

The 037's engine is a development of the long-stroke 2-liter twin-cam which powered the successful Fiat Abarth 131 rally cars, but the iron block has a new alloy cylinder head with four valves per cylinder.

Montecarlo center section

For the sake of convenience, the center section of the Lancia Beta Montecarlo is used for the 037. Competition models required the front and rear track to be wider than that on the Montecarlo. Naturally, wider bodywork had to be grafted on.

ZF transmission

Lancia's existing transmissions were not strong enough for the supercharged engine in competition spec. The more robust German ZF five-speed was used instead.

Supercharger

Lancia chose supercharging to eliminate turbo lag and get instant throttle response. Supercharging requires similar changes to turbocharging, including reducing the compression ratio.

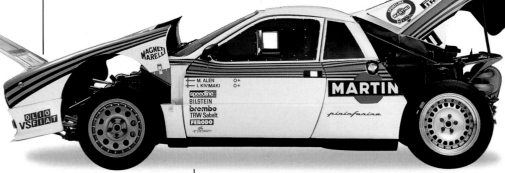

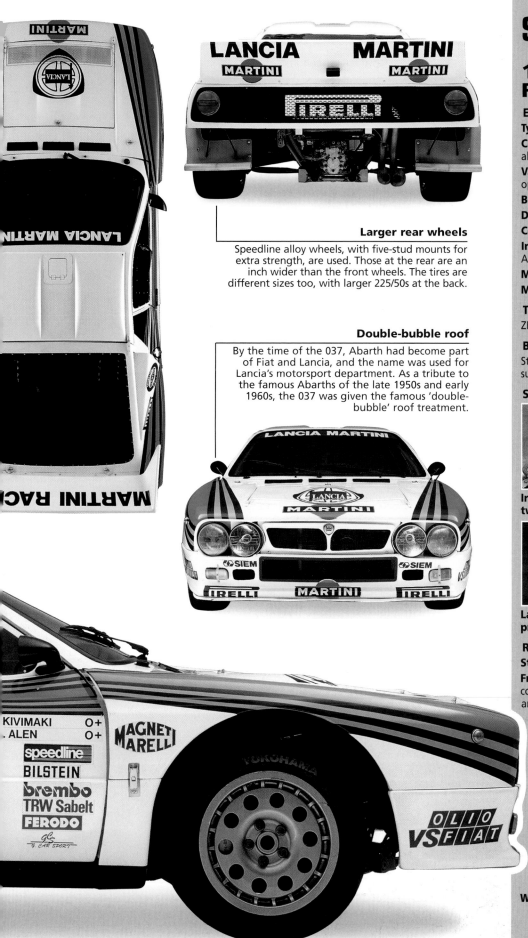

Larger rear wheels

Speedline alloy wheels, with five-stud mounts for extra strength, are used. Those at the rear are an inch wider than the front wheels. The tires are different sizes too, with larger 225/50s at the back.

Double-bubble roof

By the time of the 037, Abarth had become part of Fiat and Lancia, and the name was used for Lancia's motorsport department. As a tribute to the famous Abarths of the late 1950s and early 1960s, the 037 was given the famous 'double-bubble' roof treatment.

Specifications

1985 Lancia Rally 037 Evo 2

ENGINE
Type: In-line four

Construction: Cast-iron block and alloy cylinder head

Valve gear: Four valves per cylinder operated by twin overhead camshafts

Bore and stroke: 3.35 in. x 3.66 in.

Displacement: 2,111 cc

Compression ratio: 7.5:1

Induction system: Fuel injection with Abarth Volumex supercharger

Maximum power: 325 bhp at 8,000 rpm

Maximum torque: Not quoted

TRANSMISSION
ZF five-speed manual

BODY/CHASSIS
Steel center section with tubular-steel subframes and steel/Kevlar body

SPECIAL FEATURES

In ultimate Evo 2 form the Fiat/Lancia twin-cam engine produces 325 bhp.

Large scoops behind the side windows provide cooling air for the engine.

RUNNING GEAR
Steering: Rack-and-pinion

Front suspension: Double wishbones with coil springs, telescopic shock absorbers and anti-roll bar

Rear suspension: Double wishbones with coil springs and dual shock absorbers

Brakes: Vented discs, 11.8-in. dia. (front and rear)

Wheels: Speedline alloy, 8 x 16 in. (front), 9 x 16 in. (rear)

Tires: Pirelli P7, 205/55 VR16 (front), 225/50 VR16 (rear)

DIMENSIONS
Length: 154.1 in. **Width:** 72.8 in.

Height: 49.0 in. **Wheelbase:** 96.1 in.

Track: 59.4 in. (front), 58.7 in. (rear)

Weight: 2,117 lbs.

Lancia **THEMA 8.32**

The Thema was a competent, if uninspiring, executive sedan. When Lancia added a little Ferrari magic in the shape of the V8 from the 308, it created an ultimate street sleeper. With 215 bhp, the performance was shattering for such a sedate-looking sedan.

"...Symphony of quad cams."

"The interior suggests luxury much more than it does performance. It is only when you're speeding down the road that this car's true identity comes out. The engine's symphony of quad cams and the infamous exhaust rasp can only come from a Ferrari 3.0-liter. Despite the huge power output going through the front wheels, torque steer has been virtually eliminated. The suspension and electronically-controlled shocks give a firm ride with good handling."

The well-appointed interior gives little indication that this Thema is a Ferrari-powered road rocket.

Milestones

1984 Lancia launches its
new executive sedan, the Thema. It is a joint venture and the platform is later used for the Alfa Romeo 164, the Fiat Croma and the Saab 9000. Engines are Fiat-based twin-cam four cylinders and the PRV (Peugeot, Renault, Volvo) 2.8-liter V6.

The Thema 8.32 borrowed its engine from the Ferrari 308.

1988 The Thema V6 is dropped
from the range. However, a new model, the Thema 8.32, is launched. It uses the 3.0-liter V8 from the Ferrari 308, with 215 bhp, and has 140-mph capability.

The next most powerful Thema was the 160-bhp Turbo.

1990 Thema 8.32 production
comes to an end after only two years. Only 2,370 have been built, but its legendary status continues to impress.

UNDER THE SKIN

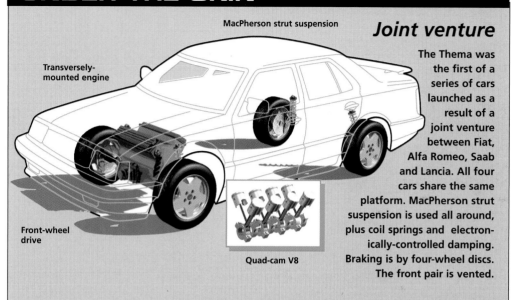

MacPherson strut suspension

Transversely-mounted engine

Front-wheel drive

Quad-cam V8

Joint venture

The Thema was the first of a series of cars launched as a result of a joint venture between Fiat, Alfa Romeo, Saab and Lancia. All four cars share the same platform. MacPherson strut suspension is used all around, plus coil springs and electronically-controlled damping. Braking is by four-wheel discs. The front pair is vented.

THE POWER PACK

Formidable Ferrari

Instead of the Fiat-based twin-cam four and the PRV V6 fitted to lesser Themas, the 8.32 uses the 3.0-liter V8 engine from the Ferrari 308. It is used in Quattrovalvole form, and is an all-alloy unit with four valves per cylinder operated by two overhead camshafts per cylinder bank. There is Marelli mapped ignition and Bosch KE3 Jetronic fuel injection. In the Ferrari 308 Quattrovalvole, this unit produced 240 bhp, but the Thema 8.32 made do with a maximum output of 215 bhp.

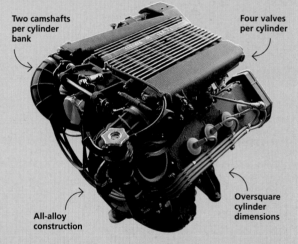

Two camshafts per cylinder bank

Four valves per cylinder

All-alloy construction

Oversquare cylinder dimensions

Street sleeper

The Thema 8.32 is perhaps the most deceptive high performer to come out of the 1980s. The Thema is handsome but not striking, and most people wouldn't give it a second look. Their heads would turn, however, when they heard its engine under full throttle.

There are few clues to the 8.32's performance potential.

Lancia **THEMA 8.32**

Before Lancia fitted the Ferrari V8, the fastest car in the Thema range was the fierce four-cylinder Turbo. By normal standards this car was quick; compared to the 8.32 it looked like it was traveling in reverse.

MacPherson strut suspension

Along with coil springs and electronically-controlled damping, the Thema uses MacPherson strut suspension at all four corners. Anti-roll bars are used front and rear.

Ferrari V8

Lancia took the quad-cam V8 from the Ferrari 308 and mounted it transversely in the front of the Thema. It produced 215 bhp—a little down on the Ferrari's 240-bhp output.

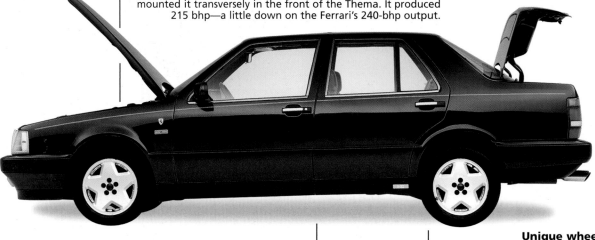

Shared platform

The Thema is built on the Type 4 platform, shared with the Alfa Romeo 164, Fiat Croma and Saab 9000.

Unique wheels

Five-spoke alloy wheels are unique to the 8.32 and help set it apart from lesser Themas.

Luxury interior

With leather and wood trim on a long list of standard equipment, the Thema 8.23's interior has more of a luxury than a sporty bias. Despite its sporty pretensions it can seat five in total comfort.

Powerful brakes

The 8.32 uses vented front and solid rear disc brakes. It also uses a three-channel anti-lock braking system.

Big trunk

The trunk has a volume of 19.3 cubic feet, but a relatively small opening restricts the size of loads that can be carried.

Specifications

1990 Lancia Thema 8.32

ENGINE

Type: V8

Construction: Alloy block and heads

Valve gear: Four valves per cylinder operated by four overhead camshafts

Bore and stroke: 3.27 in. x 2.80 in.

Displacement: 2,927 cc

Compression ratio: 10.5:1

Induction system: Bosch KE3 Jetronic fuel injection

Maximum power: 215 bhp at 6,750 rpm

Maximum torque: 210 lb-ft at 4,500 rpm

TRANSMISSION

Five-speed manual

BODY/CHASSIS

Unitary monocoque construction four-door steel sedan body

SPECIAL FEATURES

The neat trunk lid spoiler is unique to the Thema 8.32.

The Ferrari-designed V8 was built by motorcycle manufacturer Ducati.

RUNNING GEAR

Steering: Rack-and-pinion

Front suspension: MacPherson struts with coil springs, telescopic shock absorbers and anti-roll bar

Rear suspension: MacPherson struts with coil springs, telescopic shock absorbers and anti-roll bar

Brakes: Vented discs (front), solid discs (rear)

Wheels: Alloy, 6 x 15 in.

Tires: 205/55 VR15

DIMENSIONS

Length: 180.7 in. **Width:** 69.3 in.

Height: 55.9 in.   **Wheelbase:** 104.7 in.

Track: 58.7 in. (front), 58.3 in. (rear)

Weight: 3,087 lbs.

Lotus OMEGA/CARLTON

Designed to be the ultimate flagship for GM subsidiaries Vauxhall and Opel, this high-performance super sedan was easily the fastest production four-door in the world. With its twin-turbo straight-six engine it can out-accelerate a Ferrari Testarossa and has a staggering top speed.

"...huge grip and poise."

"Don't judge the Lotus Omega by its looks; just imagine it has the body of a Lamborghini. Yes, it's that fast. In 11 seconds it's hitting 100 mph. In 24 seconds you're doing 140 mph and it's still pulling hard. Even at these speeds it remains rock stable and rides well. And braking is just as incredible. The Omega's sheer size might feel a little clumsy on small roads, but on fast, open roads nothing can touch its combination of huge grip and poise."

A six-speed shifter and close-fitting bucket seats are the only notable changes inside.

Milestones

1988 GM starts
Lotus on the project that will become the Vauxhall Lotus Carlton (and the almost identical Opel Lotus Omega). The car is unveiled at the Geneva Motor Show the following March.

Back in the 1960s Lotus converted the 'cooking' Cortina Mk 1 into a legendary sports sedan.

1990 Production
begins with Carltons and Omegas transported to the Lotus factory in Hethel, where Lotus technicians install a twin-turbo straight-six engine and six-speed transmission, and modify the chassis, suspension and exterior.

Lotus used the Vauxhall Carlton/Opel Omega GSi 3000 as the basis for its 170-mph supercar.

1992 Production
ends after 950 cars have been built. GM had planned to produce 1,100, but the onset of a major recession results in a fall in demand.

UNDER THE SKIN

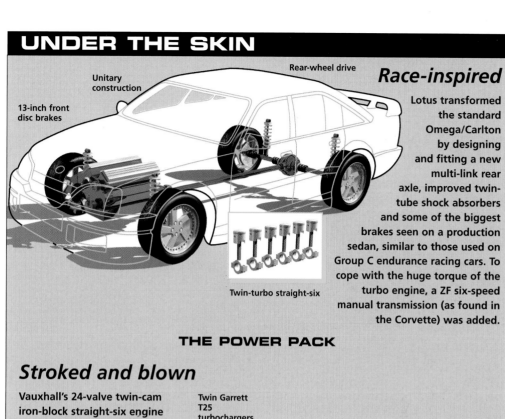

Rear-wheel drive

Unitary construction

13-inch front disc brakes

Twin-turbo straight-six

Race-inspired

Lotus transformed the standard Omega/Carlton by designing and fitting a new multi-link rear axle, improved twin-tube shock absorbers and some of the biggest brakes seen on a production sedan, similar to those used on Group C endurance racing cars. To cope with the huge torque of the turbo engine, a ZF six-speed manual transmission (as found in the Corvette) was added.

THE POWER PACK

Stroked and blown

Vauxhall's 24-valve twin-cam iron-block straight-six engine was totally revamped by Lotus. Fitting a new longer-stroke forged-steel crankshaft and Mahle forged-alloy pistons turned it into a 3.6-liter (3.74 inches x 3.35 inches) unit with a lower (8.2:1) compression ratio to withstand the forces produced by two small Garrett T25 turbochargers. They share the same intercooler and also bump power up to 377 bhp, ensuring masses of torque to move the relatively heavy Omega.

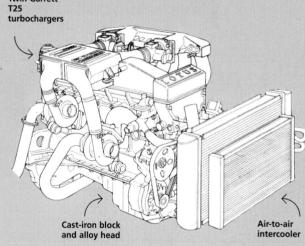

Twin Garrett T25 turbochargers

Cast-iron block and alloy head

Air-to-air intercooler

Ferrari killer

One of the best GM cars in recent years is the Lotus Omega. It offers unbelievable performance yet has five seats and a sizable trunk. A total of 510 left-hand drive Lotus Omegas were built, the rest being right-hand drive Carltons.

All cars were assembled in the UK, although most were Lotus Omegas.

Lotus OMEGA/CARLTON

The look of the Lotus Omega/Carlton suggests high performance, but this is a genuine 377-bhp twin-turbo monster which is capable of seating five people in the utmost comfort.

Twin turbos

Although the straight-six could have been fed by a single turbocharger, Lotus opted for two smaller Garrett T25 units because the smaller rotors spin faster and hence the boost comes quicker.

Lotus suspension

Although the front MacPherson strut suspension is nearly stock except for its different camber settings, the rear has extra locating links and progressive rate springs fitted.

Larger wheels

Huge 17-inch diameter forged-alloy five-spoke Ronal wheels are standard on the Lotus Omega. The front ones are 8.5 inches across and those at the rear are 9.5 inches.

Leather interior

The interior has leather upholstery and more supportive front and rear seats.

Rear spoiler

At 170 mph, downforce is of utmost importance, and huge rear spoilers are often fitted to cars capable of such speeds. The Lotus Omega, however, is an exception to this rule.

Rocker extensions

To help stability at speeds above 170 mph the Omega has special Lotus-developed rocker panel extensions to prevent excess air from getting underneath the car and causing unwanted lift.

Huge tires

The larger wheels carry ultra-low-profile 235/45 and 265/40 ZR17 tires.

Specifications

1990 Lotus Omega

ENGINE

Type: In-line six

Construction: Cast-iron block and alloy cylinder head

Valve gear: Four valves per cylinder operated by twin overhead camshafts

Bore and stroke: 3.74 in. x 3.35 in.

Displacement: 3,615 cc

Compression ratio: 8.2:1

Induction system: Electronic fuel injection with two Garrett T25 turbochargers and a single intercooler

Maximum power: 377 bhp at 5,200 rpm

Maximum torque: 419 lb-ft at 4,200 rpm

TRANSMISSION

ZF six-speed manual

BODY/CHASSIS

Unitary construction with four-door body

SPECIAL FEATURES

The word Lotus stamped on the cam cover indicates something special.

Huge scoops in the front air dam help to feed the intercooler.

RUNNING GEAR

Steering: Recirculating ball

Front suspension: MacPherson struts with anti-roll bar

Rear suspension: Multi-link with progressive rate coil springs and telescopic shock absorbers

Brakes: Vented discs, 13-in. dia. (front), solid discs, 11.8-in. dia. (rear)

Wheels: Ronal forged-alloy, 8.5 x 17 in. (front), 9.5 x 17 in. (rear)

Tires: 235/45 ZR17 (front), 265/40 ZR17 (rear)

DIMENSIONS

Length: 187.7 in.   **Width:** 76.1 in.

Height: 56.5 in.   **Wheelbase:** 107.5 in.

Track: 56.9 in. (front), 57.8 in. (rear)

Weight: 3,640 lbs.

Maserati **3500GT**

Building on the fame of its sports and racing cars like the World Championship-winning 250F, Maserati's first GT to be made in any numbers was a huge success. In seven years, more than 2,000 were sold.

"...dramatic acceleration."

"A heavy clutch and a high-strung straight-six engine suggest this is an Italian muscle car, but it's more refined than that, with a delightfully light and precise gearshift and an engine that smooths out beautifully at high rpm. It is best driven smoothly rather than thrown about—under such behavior, the great weight and low-geared steering makes the car seem undignified. It's better just to sit back and enjoy the dramatic straightline acceleration."

A large steering wheel and comprehensive instrumentation dominate the painted dash.

Milestones

1957 Maserati replaces its low-production A6 sports car with what it intends to be its first mass-produced model.

1958 The 3500GT is proving to be a success, with customers opting for either the convertible or coupe.

The Sebring shared the 3500GT's straight-six engine.

1959 Sales continue to grow, with more than 200 sold, helped by the introduction of the Girling disc brake system.

The later Maserati Mexico uses a quad-cam V8 engine.

1961 The classic system of multiple Weber carburetors is replaced by Lucas fuel injection.

1964 Production ends after 2,227 models have been built.

UNDER THE SKIN

Fabricated separate chassis

Steel and alloy body

Wishbone front suspension

In-line six

Complex chassis

In typical Italian fashion, the 3500GT has a complicated fabricated separate chassis. It is a collection of round and square tubes, with two main longitudinal members running through the engine bay back to the rear bulkhead, and another two in the sill area. It has a coil-sprung double wishbone front suspension and a live rear axle located and sprung by semi-elliptic leaf springs.

THE POWER PACK

Maserati twin-cam

Classic Italian performance twin-cam design produced an alloy block and head with the pistons carried in a fascinating version of cast-iron wet liners. Dry liners are pressed into the block but surrounded by water for the top two inches. They project up beyond the level of the head, with sealing rings to keep the coolant out and making a head gasket unnecessary. The bore size is large enough to allow twin spark plugs per cylinder, fired by twin coils.

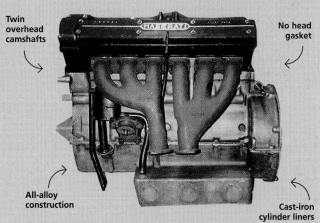

Twin overhead camshafts

No head gasket

All-alloy construction

Cast-iron cylinder liners

Super Sebring

When Vignale rebodied the 3500GT in 1963, the car became known as the Sebring. This was the best of the range, thanks to improvements like four-wheel disc brakes, a five-speed transmission and more power from a range of engines up to 4.0 liters.

The Sebring is simply a restyled 3500GTi, but it later used bigger engines.

Maserati **3500GT**

The style of the handcrafted Touring or Vignale bodies promised great performance. Appearances weren't deceptive as the superb 3.5-liter twin-cam straight-six gave 230 bhp and took the car to almost 130 mph.

Twin-cam engine

Although sometimes said to be inspired by the 250F Formula 1 engine, the 3500GT's has a number of differences. The 250's unit is a short stroke, 2.5-liter straight six with gear-driven camshafts and a very high compression ratio.

Separate chassis

Maserati used the same wheelbase as on its previous sports car but with a new chassis design made from tubular steel. It was not as complicated as the famous 'Birdcage' racer but was much more intricate than a simple ladder or perimeter frame.

ZF transmission

The 3500GT started its life with a ZF four-speed manual transmission, although later cars had the advantage of a five-speed manual, as well as the option of a Borg-Warner three-speed automatic.

Live rear axle

Maserati used the simplest of all rear suspension designs: a live axle located and sprung on very long semi-elliptic leaf springs. A single torque reaction arm, as well as an anti-roll bar, prevents axle windup.

Wishbone suspension

Double wishbone suspension was the obvious choice at the front, fitted with a concentric coil spring and telescopic shock absorber unit between the two wishbones.

Steel and alloy bodywork

Bodies for the 3500GT were made, with a few exceptions, by the famous coachbuilders Touring of Milan or Vignale, partly because they offered the right style and partly because Maserati had no facility for making the bodies, which were built in alloy and steel.

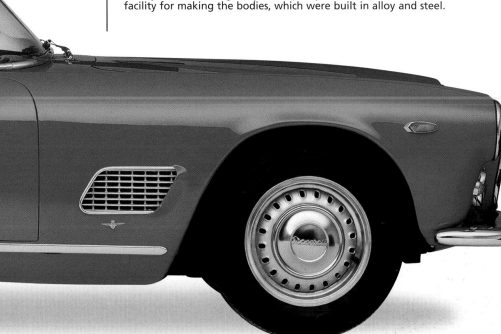

Specifications

1961 Maserati 3500GT

ENGINE

Type: In-line six-cylinder

Construction: Alloy block and head

Valve gear: Two valves per cylinder operated by chain-driven twin overhead camshafts

Bore and stroke: 3.39 in. x 3.94 in.

Displacement: 3,485 cc

Compression ratio: 8.2:1

Induction system: Lucas mechanical fuel injection

Maximum power: 230 bhp at 5,500 rpm

Maximum torque: 224 lb-ft at 4,500 rpm

TRANSMISSION

ZF four-speed manual

BODY/CHASSIS

Separate steel tube fabricated chassis with steel and alloy coupe bodywork by Touring of Milan

SPECIAL FEATURES

The 3500GT was available with these perforated steel wheels or center-lock Borrani wires.

Chrome cooling vents in the front fenders help expel hot air from the engine bay.

RUNNING GEAR

Steering: Recirculating ball

Front suspension: Double wishbones with coil springs, telescopic shock absorbers and anti-roll bar

Rear suspension: Live axle with semi-elliptic leaf springs, torque arm, telescopic shock absorbers and anti-roll bar

Brakes: Girling discs (front), drums (rear)

Wheels: Steel, 6.00 x 16 in.

Tires: 6.70-16

DIMENSIONS

Length: 185.0 in. **Width:** 63.7 in.

Height: 51.2 in. **Wheelbase:** 102.2 in.

Track: 54.7 in. (front), 53.5 in. (rear)

Weight: 3,180 lbs.

Maserati **BORA**

The Bora marked Maserati's move into the modern world in the early 1970s. It was the company's first mid-engined supercar and was designed to compete with exotic mid-engined rivals from Ferrari and Lamborghini.

"...mid-engined V8 performer."

"Almost an Italian muscle car rather than a supercar, the Bora has a lot in common with the De Tomaso, employing a big V8 engine instead of a high-revving 12 cylinder engine. The V8 has masses of torque and powers the Bora to 100 mph in just 15 seconds. The car cruises comfortably at high speeds, but its stiff springing results in a hard ride. Although it has very responsive steering, it takes a brave driver to throw the Bora around."

The Bora's interior is comfortable, but unfortunately it has hard-to-read instruments.

Milestones

1968 Citroën becomes Maserati's major shareholder and gives the firm financial strength to consider exciting new models. Maserati agrees to build two mid-engined cars, the V6 Merak and V8 Bora.

1971 The Bora makes its world debut at the Geneva Show in March, and enters production soon after.

Maserati's 4.7-liter V8 also powers the beautiful Ghibli.

1974 Long after being sold in Europe, the Bora is finally made suitable for the American market. The larger 4.9-liter V8 satisfies the more stringent emissions and safety requirements.

Smaller than the Bora, the Merak features V6 power.

1980 Production of the Bora finally comes to an end.

UNDER THE SKIN

Old and new

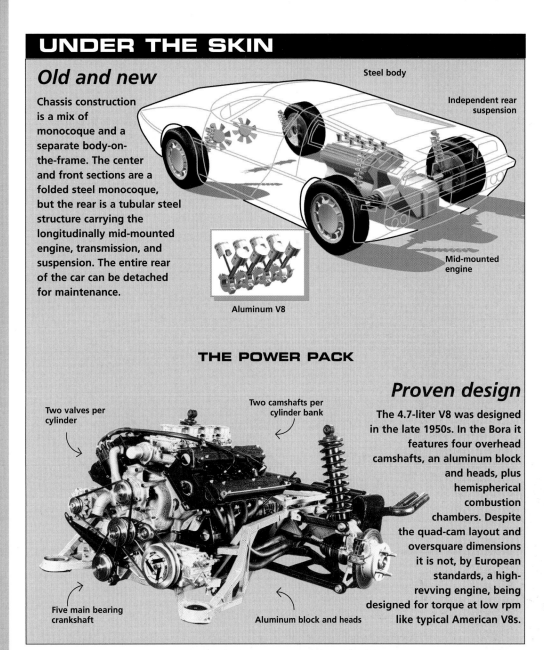

Chassis construction is a mix of monocoque and a separate body-on-the-frame. The center and front sections are a folded steel monocoque, but the rear is a tubular steel structure carrying the longitudinally mid-mounted engine, transmission, and suspension. The entire rear of the car can be detached for maintenance.

Steel body

Independent rear suspension

Mid-mounted engine

Aluminum V8

THE POWER PACK

Proven design

The 4.7-liter V8 was designed in the late 1950s. In the Bora it features four overhead camshafts, an aluminum block and heads, plus hemispherical combustion chambers. Despite the quad-cam layout and oversquare dimensions it is not, by European standards, a high-revving engine, being designed for torque at low rpm like typical American V8s.

Two valves per cylinder

Two camshafts per cylinder bank

Five main bearing crankshaft

Aluminum block and heads

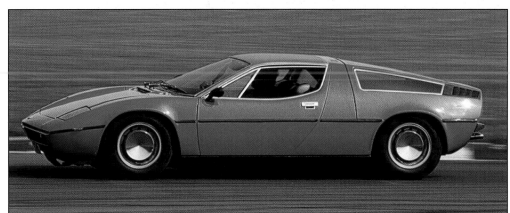

Bigger engine

In 1974 a bigger, 4.9-liter version of the V8 was used in Boras destined for the U.S. The larger engine was required to satisfy economy and emissions laws. Available in European trim from 1976, it produces 10 bhp extra and naturally offers more performance.

Although it had a long production run, only 570 Boras were built.

Maserati BORA

The Bora, which is the Italian name for a strong wind, has a slippery shape and slices through the air at speeds of up to 160 mph thanks to its 310 bhp quad-cam V8 engine.

V8 engine

The Bora's V8 engine is as large as a typical American V8 of the time but is made of alloy instead of cast-iron and has four overhead camshafts. It is a more complicated but exciting way of producing 310 bhp from 4.7 liters.

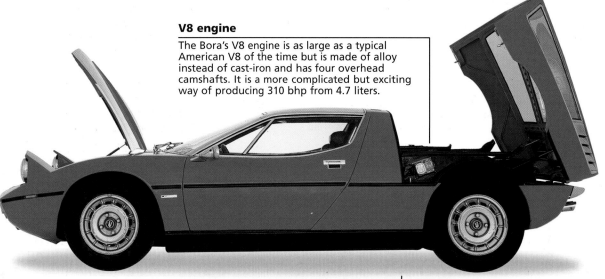

Rear subframe

At the rear, a welded-up square tube structure is used to support the engine, transmission and rear suspension.

Early alloy bodies

The very first Boras were produced with hand-crafted alloy bodies, a skill Maserati was well versed in. Standard production Boras, however, have steel bodies.

Transmission behind engine

German manufacturers ZF supplied the transmission, which is mounted behind the engine toward the tail of the car. This requires a longer and more complicated gear linkage.

Vented discs

Both front and rear brakes are discs, as is common on Italian supercars of the 1970s. They are also vented to improve cooling and to prevent fade.

Aerodynamic shape

Even though the Bora never went anywhere near a wind tunnel, designer Giorgetto Giugiaro achieved a drag coefficient of just 0.30.

Front-mounted radiator

Unlike later mid-engined cars, the Bora has a front-mounted radiator with electric fans.

Specifications

1973 Maserati Bora

ENGINE
Type: V8

Construction: Light alloy block and heads

Valve gear: Two inclined valves per cylinder operated by four chain-driven overhead camshafts via bucket tappets

Bore and stroke: 3.69 in. x 3.35 in.

Displacement: 4,719 cc

Compression ratio: 8.5:1

Induction system: Four Weber DCNF/14 downdraft carburetors

Maximum power: 310 bhp at 6,000 rpm

Maximum torque: 325 lb-ft at 4,200 rpm

TRANSMISSION
Five-speed ZF manual

BODY/CHASSIS
Steel unitary construction front sections with square-tube rear frame; steel two-door coupe body

SPECIAL FEATURES

The flat rear end or 'Kamm tail' was a popular feature on 1970s supercars.

The Bora was an early Giorgetto Giugiaro design.

RUNNING GEAR
Steering: Rack-and-pinion

Front suspension: Double wishbones with coil springs, telescopic shocks and anti-roll bar

Rear suspension: Double wishbones with coil springs, telescopic shocks and anti-roll bar

Brakes: Vented discs (front and rear), with Citroën high-pressure hydraulics

Wheels: Alloy, 7.5 in. x 15 in.

Tires: Michelin 215/70 VR15

DIMENSIONS
Length: 170.4 in.   **Width:** 68.1 in.

Height: 44.6 in.   **Wheelbase:** 102 in.

Track: 58 in. (front), 57 in. (rear)

Weight: 3,570 lbs.

Maserati KHAMSIN

Named after a warm, fast wind, the Khamsin was a sharp-suited supercar that lived up to the speed that its name implied. To many eyes it was the last great Maserati coupe before the firm was taken over by De Tomaso.

"...lightning-quick steering."

"The Khamsin is a little intimidating when you first drive it. It feels like a large car and the quirky hydraulic systems behave differently than anything but a Citroën. The really enjoyable part is the engine, with its glorious soundtrack. Considering it is hauling almost two tons, its performance is remarkably strong. The lightning-quick steering helps you coax the Khamsin around corners. Poise is superb, although the trade-off is a rather lumpy ride."

The switch-packed dashboard is typical of an Italian supercar, and the design has flair.

Milestones

1973 Visitors to the Paris
Motor Show are treated to Maserati's vision of a range-topping GT car, the Khamsin.

A replacement for the Khamsin, the V8 Indy was Maserati's first-ever unit-construction car.

1974 Alongside the Merak
coupe, the Khamsin takes on a key role in Maserati's range when its forerunner, the Indy, is discontinued. A worthy successor, the Khamsin soon becomes popular.

1975 Citroën, the major shareholder,
puts Maserati into liquidation, but the marque is rescued by De Tomaso.

The Merak was sold alongside the Khamsin through the 1970s.

1982 Steady demand has
kept the Khamsin in production for nine years. Maserati is entering the Biturbo era, however, and a change of direction is needed. As a result, the big GT is put out to pasture.

UNDER THE SKIN

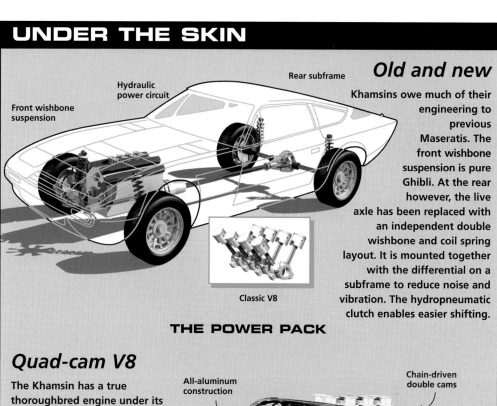

Hydraulic power circuit

Rear subframe

Front wishbone suspension

Classic V8

Old and new

Khamsins owe much of their engineering to previous Maseratis. The front wishbone suspension is pure Ghibli. At the rear however, the live axle has been replaced with an independent double wishbone and coil spring layout. It is mounted together with the differential on a subframe to reduce noise and vibration. The hydropneumatic clutch enables easier shifting.

THE POWER PACK

Quad-cam V8

The Khamsin has a true thoroughbred engine under its hood. Unlike the modern Biturbo engines, the Khamsin's 4.9-liter V8 is the ultimate expression of the classic Maserati V8 bloodline that began in 1963 with the Quattroporte. Its capacity of 4,930 cc is shared with the great Maserati Ghibli SS, and it is an incredibly under-stressed engine. Of all-aluminum construction and with five main bearings, it features chain-driven double overhead camshafts on each bank of cylinders.

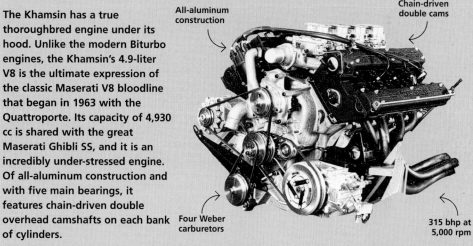

All-aluminum construction

Chain-driven double cams

Four Weber carburetors

315 bhp at 5,000 rpm

Thoroughbred

It is true that the Khamsin will never approach the seminal Ghibli of the 1960s in classic Maserati terms, but that does have one advantage. The Khamsin can be bought for a bargain price compared to earlier Maseratis, yet it has all the Ghibli's ability.

The shape is classic Maserati, but prices are not as daunting as they might be.

Maserati KHAMSIN

The Khamsin was conceived when Citroën held the strings at Maserati and the French firm's influence can be seen in the numerous hydraulic circuits. It may be complex, but this is one of the most charismatic Maseratis built.

Pop up headlights

Even the pop up headlights are raised and lowered by the hydraulic system that powers the brakes, steering and clutch. The driver's seat is also adjusted using the same circuit.

Self-centering steering

The rack-and-pinion steering uses hydraulic assistance to provide ultra-sensitive feel. A unique feature is its self-centering steering system that increases with speed.

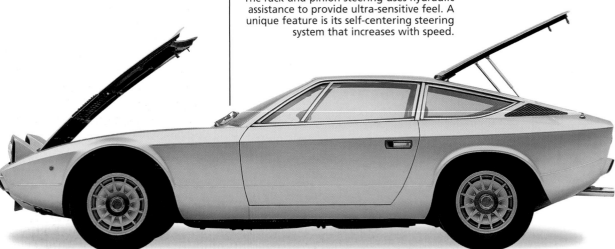

All-independent suspension

Abandoning a live rear axle, the Khamsin was the first front-engined Maserati to gain all-around independent suspension. It uses upper and lower wishbones with two sets of springs per side, all mounted on a separate subframe.

2+2 interior

The small rear seats are extremely tight and are practically useless except for small children. However, a large rear hatch opens up to reveal a generous trunk area.

Asymmetric cooling

The hood incorporates three louvers for engine cooling. The main one is positioned asymmetrically as a distinctive styling feature.

Citroën hydraulics

A strong part of the Khamsin's character comes from its Citroën hydraulic system. This consists of separate pumps that keep an oleo-pneumatic circuit charged up to high pressure, providing all the power assistance for the controls, including the steering, brakes and clutch.

Specifications

1975 Maserati Khamsin

ENGINE

Type: V8

Construction: Aluminum block and heads

Valve gear: Two valves per cylinder operated by double chain-driven overhead camshafts

Bore and stroke: 3.70 in. x 3.50 in.

Displacement: 4,930 cc

Compression ratio: 8:1

Induction system: Four Weber carburetors

Maximum power: 315 bhp at 5,000 rpm

Maximum torque: 308 lb-ft at 4,000 rpm

TRANSMISSION

Five-speed manual or three-speed automatic

BODY/CHASSIS

Unitary monocoque construction chassis with steel two-door coupe body

SPECIAL FEATURES

The twin pop up headlights are operated by the Citroën-produced hydraulic system.

The trunk lid and fuel filler flap are operated by levers in the door jamb.

RUNNING GEAR

Steering: Rack-and-pinion

Front suspension: Unequal length wishbones with coil springs, shock absorbers and anti-roll bar

Rear suspension: Unequal length wishbones with dual coil springs, shock absorbers and anti-roll bar

Brakes: Discs (front and rear)

Wheels: Alloy, 15-in. dia.

Tires: 215/70 VR15

DIMENSIONS

Length: 180.0 in.   **Width:** 71.0 in.

Height: 47.0 in.   **Wheelbase:** 100.3 in.

Track: 56.6 in. (front), 57.7 in. (rear)

Weight: 3,735 lbs.

Maserati **MERAK**

As an answer to Ferrari's highly successful Dino, Maserati produced the V6 Merak. It was an unusual sports car but was extraordinarily handsome and solid as well.

"...sharp oversteer."

"The gutsy V6 engine behind you may not have sounded as good as a Ferrari powerplant, but it does provide good acceleration. The gearing allows for very comfortable cruising as well as spirited 0-60 mph acceleration. The strangest thing about driving it is the on-off brake feel, which takes some getting used to. Handling is typical of a mid-engined car: initial understeer followed by sharp oversteer can be controlled with power, but it's tricky to drive at the limit."

Well trimmed seats and creature comforts make the cabin a pleasant environment.

Milestones

1972 Maserati launches the Merak, a junior version of its Bora supercar.

The Citroën SM shared parts with the Merak including the V6 and transmission.

1975 As Citroën pulls out of Maserati, Alejandro De Tomaso steps in. A more powerful Merak SS with a 220 bhp engine is released. Other changes include the adoption of the Bora's dash for all Meraks.

The Merak was based on the V8 powered Bora and shared its inner structure.

1980 The Merak is withdrawn from the U.S. market.

1982 Production of the Bora ends though some leftover cars continue to be sold into 1983.

UNDER THE SKIN

Bora basis

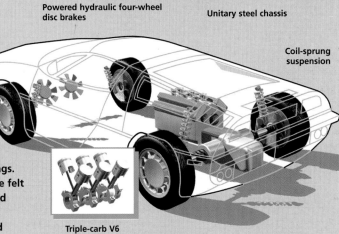

Powered hydraulic four-wheel disc brakes

Unitary steel chassis

Coil-sprung suspension

Triple-carb V6

The structure of the Merak from the roof forward was inherited from the V8 Bora, which meant a steel unitary chassis with a rear subframe, and Ingeniere Alfieri 's superb all-independent suspension by wishbones and coil springs. The Citroen influence can be felt in the hydraulically operated power clutch and braking systems, plus the five-speed transmission, which was also shared with the Citroen SM.

THE POWER PACK

Under the influence

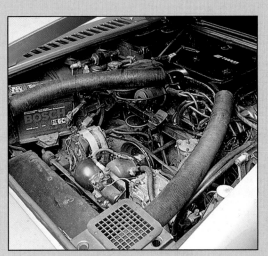

When the Merak was conceived, Maserati was owned by Citroën, which dictated the choice of powerplant: the V6 from SM, which was effectively a Maserati engine with two cylinders and a slice off the end. With a displacement of 2,965 cc, triple carburetors and dual overhead camshafts per bank, it's certainly a potent powerplant, developing 190 bhp (182 bhp in the U.S. due to strict emissions controls). A more powerful V6 arrived in 1974 in Europe, as part of the Merak SS. With bigger carburetors and a higher 9.0:1 compression ratio it produced a healthy 220 bhp. In Italy, an affordable 1,999-cc V6 engine with 159 bhp was offered.

SS supercar

The more powerful, and rarer, SS version is the most desirable for collectors and driving enthusiasts. It elevates this small rocket ship into true junior supercar territory rather than being merely a swift sports car.

The sporty Merak SS offers buyers excellent value.

Maserati MERAK

At a time when Maserati was owned by Citroën, the Merak made commercial sense. Using the Bora as its basis and the engine from the Citroën SM, a new sports car could be created for an affordable price.

Citroën-Maserati drivetrain

The V6 engine developed by Maserati for Citroën's SM was used in the Merak, albeit rotated through 90 degrees and mounted longitudinally in the center. All Meraks used a five-speed transmission shared with the SM.

ItalDesign styling

Giugiaro's ItalDesign carrozzeria designed the Bora, on which the Merak was based. Maserati asked Giugiaro to make some changes for the Merak, including a flat rear engine cover, flying rear buttresses, vertical rear window and inset front bumperettes.

Four-wheel disc brakes

Naturally, the Merak had four-wheel disc brakes; the rear pair were mounted inboard. The brakes were power-assisted using a Citroën-patented oleo-pneumatic charging system, giving a dramatic on-off feel.

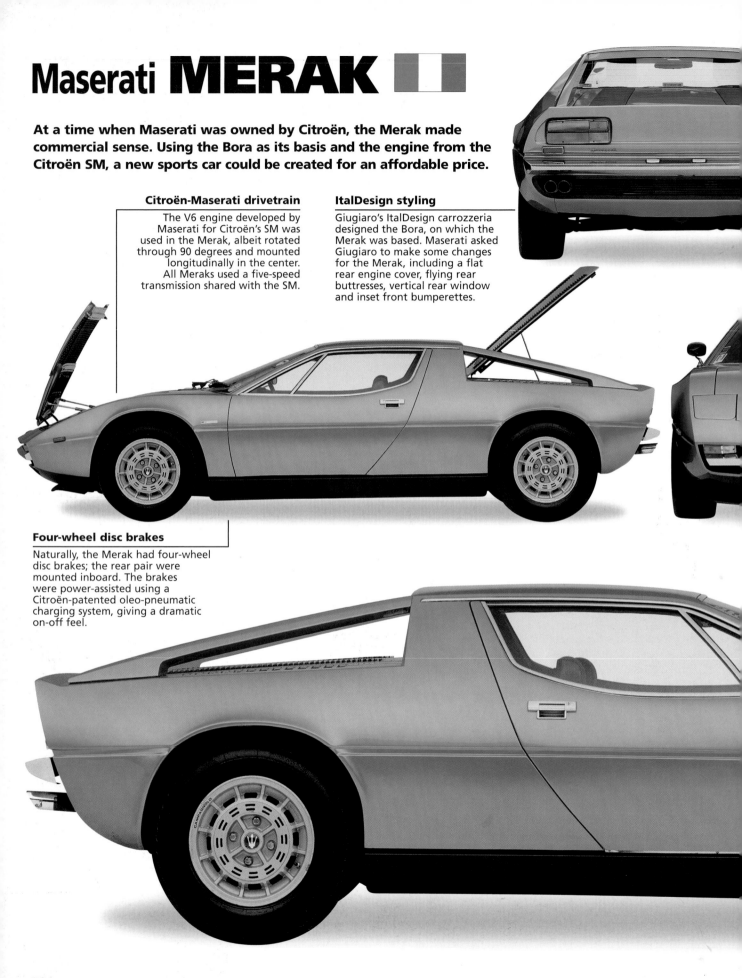

Concealed headlights

Like the Bora, the Merak features pop-up headlights. This enabled a low nose profile while at the same time satisfying height requirements for lighting in the U.S.

2+2 accommodation

Officially, the Merak is classed as a 2+2, unlike the strictly two-seater Bora. However, the packaging restrictions of the midmounted engine mean that space in the rear is extremely tight, even for children.

Citroën hydraulics

The Merak was designed around certain Citroën hydraulic components, including the clutch and brakes. The result was quite an unusual driving experience compared to other Italian exotics of the 1970s.

Specifications

1977 Maserati Merak SS

ENGINE

Type: V6

Construction: Aluminum block and heads

Valve gear: Two valves per cylinder operated by chain-driven dual overhead camshafts

Bore and stroke: 3.61 in. x 2.95 in.

Displacement: 2,965 cc

Compression ratio: 8.5:1

Induction system: Three Weber 44DNCF carburetors

Maximum power: 182 bhp at 6,000 rpm

Maximum torque: 180 lb-ft at 4,000 rpm

TRANSMISSION

Five-speed manual

BODY/CHASSIS

Unitary monocoque construction with steel two-door coupe body

SPECIAL FEATURES

Because the nose has a low, wedged shape, the headlights had to pop up to reach regulation height.

The long and angled side glass styling is all part of the Merak's appeal.

RUNNING GEAR

Steering: Rack-and-pinion

Front suspension: Double wishbones with coil springs, shock absorbers and anti-roll bar

Rear suspension: Double wishbones with coil springs, shock absorbers and anti-roll bar

Brakes: Discs (front and rear)

Wheels: Alloy, 15-in. dia.

Tires: 205/70 (front), 215/70 (rear)

DIMENSIONS

Length: 180.0 in.   **Width:** 69.6 in.

Height: 44.6 in.   **Wheelbase:** 102.3 in.

Track: 58.0 in. (front), 56.9 in. (rear)

Weight: 3,185 lbs.

Maserati MEXICO

The Mexico is so rare, it's almost the forgotten Maserati. Named after one of the Cooper Maserati's few victories, the Mexico is a generous 2+2 rather than a sports car, even though it has a near 300-bhp V8 engine.

"...perfectly tractable."

"The V8 sounds great and is perfectly tractable and comfortable at low speeds or screaming under full throttle. Acceleration is fierce for such a heavy car and easy to shift through its very direct ZF five-speed transmission. The steering is quick enough to catch the tail, which tends to slide out under hard acceleration when exiting corners or lifting off the throttle sharply. It also gives a very comfortable ride."

The Mexico's wood-trimmed interior has the classy and sporty feel that is synonymous with Maserati.

Milestones

1965 Maserati unveils a prototype
two-door, four-seat version of the Quattroporte with elegant Vignale bodywork.

The Mexico was based on the larger four-door Quattroporte.

1966 Production gets underway.
The company celebrates John Surtees' win at the Mexican Grand Prix in a Cooper-Maserati by calling the car the Mexico. The first cars have 4.7-liter, V8 engines.

The torque-happy Ghibli used the same 4.7-liter engine.

1967 The Mexico is available
with a smaller, 290-bhp, 4.2-liter V8.

1971 Maserati exhibits
a Mexico at both the Geneva and Paris Motor Shows, even though production has almost dried up, hinting that unsold cars are still available. When every one is finally sold, production has totaled 250.

UNDER THE SKIN

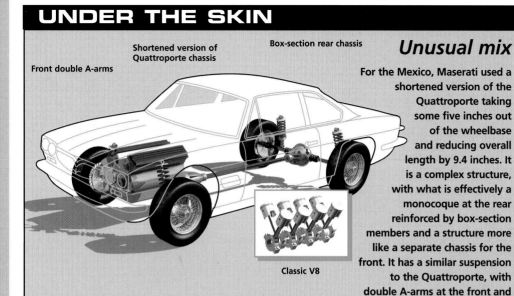

Front double A-arms

Shortened version of Quattroporte chassis

Box-section rear chassis

Classic V8

Unusual mix

For the Mexico, Maserati used a shortened version of the Quattroporte taking some five inches out of the wheelbase and reducing overall length by 9.4 inches. It is a complex structure, with what is effectively a monocoque at the rear reinforced by box-section members and a structure more like a separate chassis for the front. It has a similar suspension to the Quattroporte, with double A-arms at the front and a live rear axle.

THE POWER PACK

Racing bred

Maserati's great V8 was developed from its racing engine of the 1950s, and its exotic specification shows this off. The engine is all alloy with the pistons running in cast-iron wet liners and topped by two alloy cylinder heads. These hold twin chain-driven camshafts that open two large angled valves per cylinder in hemispherical combustion chambers with large bucket lifters. Initially a 4.7-liter engine was available, but from 1968, a smaller 4.2-liter V8 version was offered as an option.

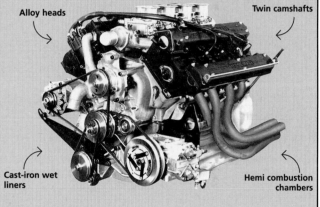

Alloy heads

Twin camshafts

Cast-iron wet liners

Hemi combustion chambers

Little brother

There was a more affordable 260-bhp, 4.2-liter V8 model produced to try to increase its slow sales. Although the car was extremely heavy, it was also still fast and had very sporty aspirations; Maserati claimed a top speed that almost hit 150 mph.

Despite the reduced power, the 4.2-liter Mexico is still a lot of fun.

Maserati MEXICO

Styled by Vignale, the body on the Mexico is perhaps just too elongated in profile. It looks its best from the front three-quarter angle, where it radiates elegance and style.

Quattroporte chassis

The Mexico is based on the chassis of the Quattroporte. It uses a combination of a sheet metal and box-section reinforced rear section with a traditional Italian style of chassis frame at the front to carry the engine and front suspension.

V8 engine

Maserati's quad-cam V8 is a magnificent engine in either 4.2- or 4.7-liter form, and it is sufficiently light for the Mexico to have perfectly equal weight distribution. It is also very strong, powerful, and reliable and was used in Maserati road cars from the early 1960s right into the 1980s.

Borrani wheels

Mexicos are normally equipped with elegant and extremely expensive Borrani wire-spoke wheels with quick-release knock-on/off spinners. At 7 x 15 inches, they were regarded as large wheels at the time. Alloy wheels were a factory option.

Optional automatic

Because it is a Grand Tourer, Maserati offered the Mexico with an optional three-speed automatic transmission. Like the ZF five-speed manual, it was bought in—from Borg-Warner—and top gear was a direct 1:1 ratio.

Wishbone front suspension

The Mexico has a classic high-performance front suspension system with double A-arms, coil springs and telescopic shock absorbers, as well as a substantial anti-roll bar.

Live rear axle

Although Maserati had produced a de Dion axle for the Quattroporte, by the time the Mexico appeared, it was using a more conventional live axle. This is suspended on semi-elliptic leaf springs.

Specifications

1968 Maserati Mexico

ENGINE

Type: V8

Construction: Alloy block with cast-iron wet liners and alloy heads

Valve gear: Two valves per cylinder operated by twin chain-driven overhead camshafts per bank of cylinders

Bore and stroke: 3.70 in. x 3.35 in.

Displacement: 4,719 cc

Compression ratio: 8.5:1

Induction system: Four Weber 42 DCNF downdraft carburetors

Maximum power: 290 bhp at 5,000 rpm

Maximum torque: 290 lb-ft at 3,800 rpm

TRANSMISSION

Five-speed manual

BODY/CHASSIS

Tubular steel chassis with Vignale steel two-door 2+2 body

SPECIAL FEATURES

The trident emblem on the grill of the Mexico is fixed to all Maseratis.

Flush-mounted door handles are a stylish piece of detail design.

RUNNING GEAR

Steering: Recirculating-ball

Front suspension: Double A-arms with coil springs, telescopic shock absorbers and anti-roll bar

Rear suspension: Live axle with trailing arms, Panhard rod, semi-elliptic leaf springs and telescopic shock absorbers

Brakes: Vented discs, 11.5-in. dia. (front), discs, 12.5-in. dia. (rear)

Wheels: Borrani wire, 7 x 15 in.

Tires: 205 x 15

DIMENSIONS

Length: 187.4 in.   **Width:** 68.1 in.

Height: 53.2 in.   **Wheelbase:** 103.9 in.

Track: 54.7 in. (front), 53.5 in. (rear)

Weight: 3,308 lbs.

Maserati **MISTRAL**

In the early 1960s, although overshadowed by Ferrari and lacking the charisma of the Maranello marques' V12 engines, Maserati still produced real thoroughbreds like the stylish Mistral.

"...ample character."

"On the road, the Mistral owes few apologies to Ferrari or anyone else. It is a practical car, with lazy performance, a fine chassis and ample character. The injection has a 'choke' for starting, which needs care, but once warmed up the six is untemperamental and flexible. The ZF transmission has a delightfully short throw and the steering is pleasantly light, though a little low geared. In reality, the Mistral is more like a grand tourer than a sports car."

The cockpit is light, spacious and luxurious, with leather upholstery and wool carpets.

Milestones

1963 Maserati previews

the Mistral at the Turin Motor Show— only 15 years after the first 'production' Maserati was introduced at the same venue.

The later Bora adopted a mid-mounted V8 engine.

1964 The Mistral reaches

the showroom floor in coupe and convertible forms. In the first year of production, Maserati sells 99 coupes and 17 convertible Spyders, which were launched at the Geneva Motor Show.

AC's 428 grand tourer was also styled by Frua.

1966 The engine's capacity

is enlarged from 3.7 to 4.0 liters. It produces 255 bhp and has even more impressive flexibility.

1970 The last three Mistrals

are sold. The model is replaced by the V8-engined Mexico and Ghibli family.

UNDER THE SKIN

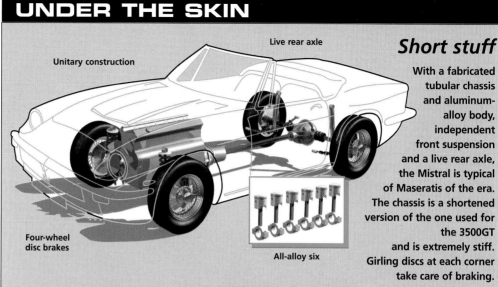

Unitary construction

Live rear axle

Four-wheel disc brakes

All-alloy six

Short stuff

With a fabricated tubular chassis and aluminum-alloy body, independent front suspension and a live rear axle, the Mistral is typical of Maseratis of the era. The chassis is a shortened version of the one used for the 3500GT and is extremely stiff. Girling discs at each corner take care of braking.

THE POWER PACK

Ultimate engine

The ultimate development of Maserati's long-stroke twin-cam straight-six, designed by Giulio Alfieri, is used in the Mistral. It is an all-alloy unit with cast-iron cylinder liners and a fully-machined crankshaft running in seven main bearings. The twin-overhead camshafts are chain-driven and operate two large valves in each hemispherical combustion chamber. There are two spark plugs per cylinder, which fire simultaneously to maximize combustion.

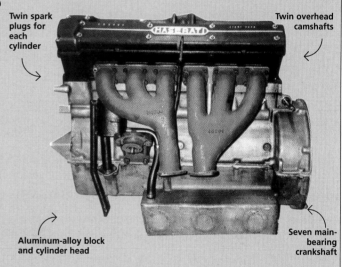

Twin spark plugs for each cylinder

Twin overhead camshafts

Aluminum-alloy block and cylinder head

Seven main-bearing crankshaft

Undervalued

Although it was in production for seven years, only 1,068 Mistrals left the factory. It is a stylish, fast, forgiving and practical car, but the Mistral is underrated. The most desirable model is the Spyder, of which only 120 were built.

Stylish and fast, the Mistral is relatively cheap to buy.

Maserati MISTRAL ▮▮

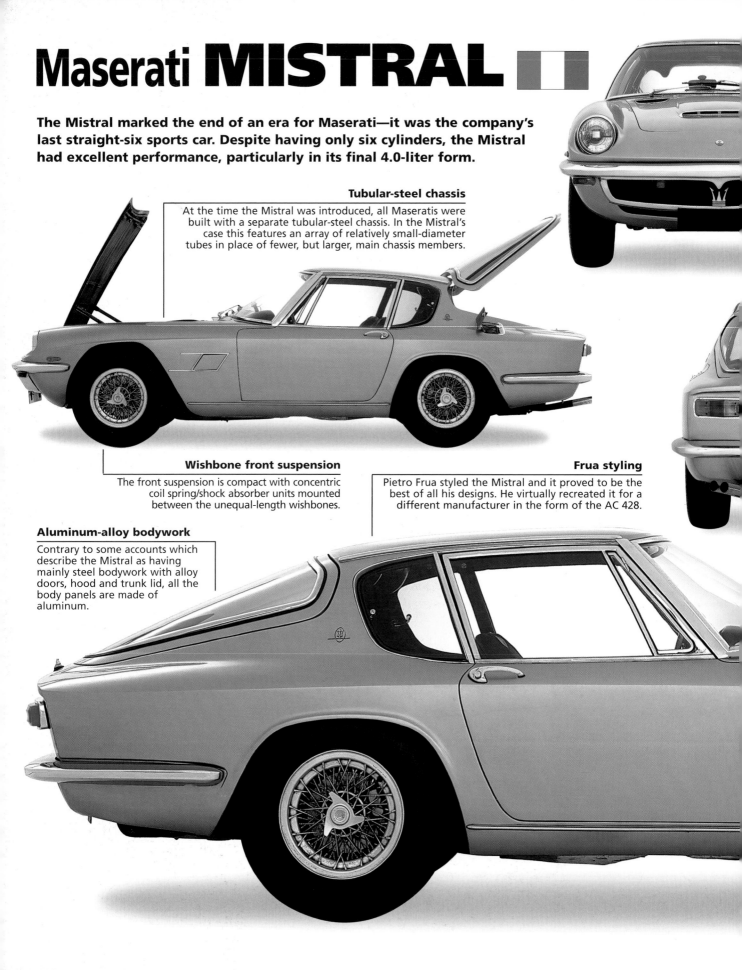

The Mistral marked the end of an era for Maserati—it was the company's last straight-six sports car. Despite having only six cylinders, the Mistral had excellent performance, particularly in its final 4.0-liter form.

Tubular-steel chassis

At the time the Mistral was introduced, all Maseratis were built with a separate tubular-steel chassis. In the Mistral's case this features an array of relatively small-diameter tubes in place of fewer, but larger, main chassis members.

Wishbone front suspension

The front suspension is compact with concentric coil spring/shock absorber units mounted between the unequal-length wishbones.

Frua styling

Pietro Frua styled the Mistral and it proved to be the best of all his designs. He virtually recreated it for a different manufacturer in the form of the AC 428.

Aluminum-alloy bodywork

Contrary to some accounts which describe the Mistral as having mainly steel bodywork with alloy doors, hood and trunk lid, all the body panels are made of aluminum.

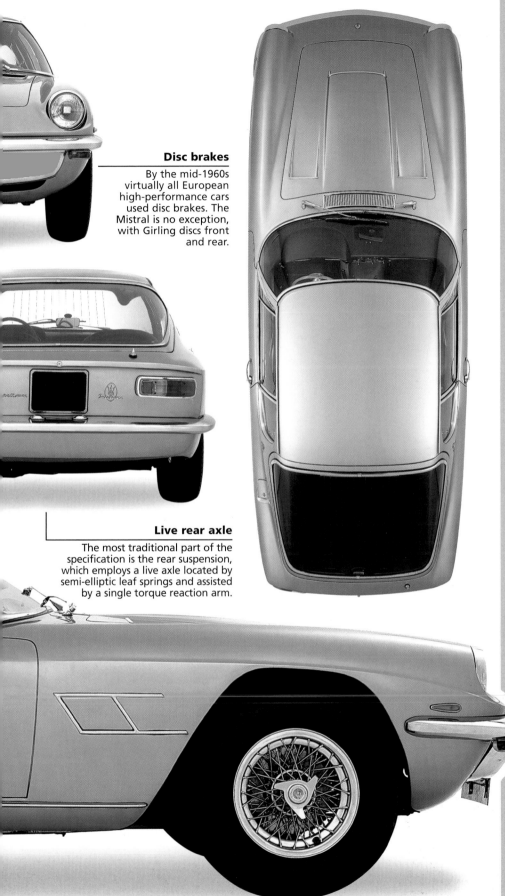

Disc brakes

By the mid-1960s virtually all European high-performance cars used disc brakes. The Mistral is no exception, with Girling discs front and rear.

Live rear axle

The most traditional part of the specification is the rear suspension, which employs a live axle located by semi-elliptic leaf springs and assisted by a single torque reaction arm.

Specifications

1967 Maserati Mistral

ENGINE

Type: In-line six

Construction: Aluminum-alloy block and head

Valve gear: Two valves per cylinder operated by two chain-driven overhead camshafts via bucket tappets and shims

Bore and stroke: 3.46 in. x 4.33 in.

Displacement: 4,014 cc

Compression ratio: 8.8:1

Induction system: Lucas mechanical fuel injection

Maximum power: 255 bhp at 5,200 rpm

Maximum torque: 267 lb-ft at 3,500 rpm

TRANSMISSION

ZF five-speed manual

BODY/CHASSIS

Tubular-steel chassis with coupe or convertible aluminum-alloy body

SPECIAL FEATURES

Tear-drop marker lights supplement the main units under the bumper.

The scoop in the fender is mechanically-operated, allowing cool air into the car.

RUNNING GEAR

Steering: Recirculating ball

Front suspension: Double wishbones with coil springs, telescopic shock absorbers and anti-roll bar

Rear suspension: Live axle with semi-elliptic leaf springs, telescopic shock absorbers, single torque reaction arm and anti-roll bar

Brakes: Discs, 12.05-in. dia. (front), 11.5-in. dia (rear)

Wheels: Borrani wire, 7 x 15 in.

Tires: 225/70 VR15

DIMENSIONS

Length: 177.2 in. **Width:** 64.9 in.

Height: 49.2 in. **Wheelbase:** 94.5 in.

Track: 54.7 in. (front), 53.3 in. (rear)

Weight: 2,866 lbs.

Maserati SEBRING

The Sebring was Maserati's way of giving a new lease on life to its popular 3500GT. With modern bodywork, more powerful engines and a five-speed transmission, the customers loved the Sebring.

"...high speed stability."

"A shorter wheelbase gives the Sebring better handling than the outgoing 3500GT. It has a well-balanced, neutral tendency, and it needs a heavy right foot to cause oversteer. High-speed stability is impressive, as is the ride at all speeds. The springs are very stiff and give it exceptionally good body control. Four-wheel discs provide excellent braking—essential when you can hit 120 mph in only 30 seconds and the top speed is nearly 140 mph."

A classic three-spoke steering wheel sets off the well-stocked dashboard.

Milestones

1957 Maserati introduces the 3500GT
as its first real mass-production sports coupe.

The 3500GT catapulted Maserati into the supercar league.

1961 The 3500GT is
improved with a standard five-speed transmission and Lucas fuel injection in place of carburetors.

Styled by Frua, the Mistral used the Sebring's straight-six engine.

1963 New Vignale bodywork
is different enough to call for a name change. Maserati chooses Sebring after the Florida race circuit. Power comes from 3.5-, 3.7- and 4.0-liter straight-six units.

1966 Sebring production
ends after 438 cars have been built. By this time the more glamourous Ghibli has taken over.

UNDER THE SKIN

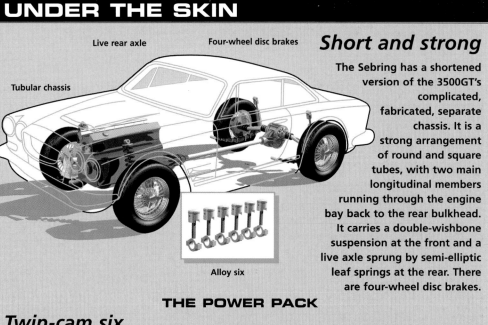

Tubular chassis · Live rear axle · Four-wheel disc brakes

Alloy six

Short and strong

The Sebring has a shortened version of the 3500GT's complicated, fabricated, separate chassis. It is a strong arrangement of round and square tubes, with two main longitudinal members running through the engine bay back to the rear bulkhead. It carries a double-wishbone suspension at the front and a live axle sprung by semi-elliptic leaf springs at the rear. There are four-wheel disc brakes.

THE POWER PACK

Twin-cam six

With this six-cylinder engine, Maserati did things differently. There is an alloy block and head, but the pistons run in an unusual form of cast-iron wet liners. These are solidly fitted in most of the block but surrounded by water for the top two inches. They project beyond the top of the block and are given sealing rings to keep the coolant out and make a head gasket unnecessary. There are twin spark plugs per cylinder for improved combustion, fired by a single distributor and twin coils.

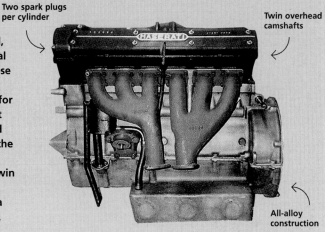

Two spark plugs per cylinder · Twin overhead camshafts · All-alloy construction

Full bore

The most exciting Sebrings are the later versions with stretched six-cylinder, twin-cam engines that displace 4.0 liters. This gives it 255 bhp, which is enough to take the top speed to 146 mph in an attempt to match rivals Ferrari and Lamborghini.

The biggest 4.0-liter Sebring is by far the fastest of the entire range.

Maserati SEBRING

Vignale's compact body made the Sebring look much more modern than the 3500GT thanks to features like its four-headlight front end and its sharper, more distinct lines.

Recirculating ball steering

It was not until the 1970s that Maserati saw the benefit of using rack-and-pinion steering. It claimed that perfectly good results could be achieved with the theoretically inferior recirculating ball arrangement.

Twin-cam engine

The all-alloy, six-cylinder, twin-cam engine was basically carried over from the 3500GT. It is a long-stroke design, just as happy to turn over gently at around 700 rpm as it is to accelerate past 6,000 rpm, which was partly a feature of the advanced fuel injection.

Steel and alloy wheels

Sebrings could be ordered with either Borrani wire-spoke, knock-on wheels or discs. Like the Borranis the steel disc wheels actually had steel centers with alloy rims for lightness.

Live axle

The rear suspension is a simple live axle suspended on semi-elliptic leaf springs, but Maserati made sure it is well located with a torque reaction arm as well as an anti-roll bar and shock absorbers angled inward toward the differential.

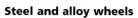

Shorter wheelbase

The Sebring is built on a chassis similar to the 3500GT but with a 3.9-inch shorter wheelbase. This helped to make it slightly more agile.

Specifications

1964 Maserati Sebring

ENGINE

Type: Inline six-cylinder

Construction: Alloy block and head

Valve gear: Two valves per cylinder operated by twin overhead camshafts

Bore and stroke: 3.38 in. x 3.94 in.

Displacement: 3,485 cc

Compression ratio: 8.8:1

Induction system: Lucas mechanical fuel injection

Maximum power: 235 bhp at 5,500 rpm

Maximum torque: 232 lb-ft at 4,000 rpm

TRANSMISSION

ZF five-speed manual

BODY/CHASSIS

Separate fabricated steel-tube chassis with steel coupe bodywork by Vignale

SPECIAL FEATURES

Fender vents behind the front wheels vent hot air from the disc brakes.

The subtle hood scoop gives the Sebring a more muscular look.

RUNNING GEAR

Steering: Recirculating ball

Front suspension: Double wishbones with coil springs, telescopic shock absorbers and anti-roll bar

Rear suspension: Live axle with semi-elliptic leaf springs, torque arm, telescopic shock absorbers and anti-roll bar

Brakes: Girling discs (front and rear)

Wheels: Borrani wires, 6.5 x 16 in.

Tires: Pirelli Cinturato, 185 x 16

DIMENSIONS

Length: 176.0 in.   **Width:** 65.3 in.

Height: 52.0 in.   **Wheelbase:** 98.5 in.

Track: 54.7 in. (front), 53.5 in (rear)

Weight: 3,335 lbs.

Nissan **300ZX TURBO**

Using the Porsche 944 Turbo as its target, Japanese giant Nissan set to transform the image of its cumbersome 300ZX—a task in which it succeeded. The new model was one of the fastest and best-handling sports cars of its day.

"...smooth, luxurious and fast."

"It's 1969, and you're driving the original 240ZX, a pure, hard-edged sports car that will inspire thousands of enthusiasts and produce a highly collectible classic. By 1984, the Z car is suffering from middle-age bloat, so a new team of experts cooks up a leaner, meaner, tastier dish. Now it's 1990, and the cult of the Z car has been recaptured with the 300ZX. You've got advanced four-wheel steering, twin intercooled turbos, plus a 20 percent stiffer 'box. It's smooth, luxurious and fast—but not as pure as the original."

Often described as the "Japanese Corvette," the feel of 300ZX cockpit is purposeful and refined.

Milestones

1984 The line that started with the original 240Z in 1969 culminates in the bloated and ugly 300ZX—it was time for a fundamental change. Nissan creates a new project team to go back to basics and design a world-beating Z car for the 1990s.

Nissan's new 300ZX Turbo was blisteringly fast, and had the braking to match.

1989 New 300ZX is launched on the vital American market after making its world debut in February at the Chicago Motor Show.

At last Nissan's Z car had a chassis to match its great performance.

1990 The 300ZX becomes available in Europe.

1992 To broaden the car's appeal a two-seater convertible is introduced, unveiled at the Detroit Motor Show, showing how important the North American market continues to be for Nissan.

UNDER THE SKIN

Computer designed

The suspension sets the Nissan apart. With the help of two huge Cray supercomputers, double-wishbone suspension was developed to complement the four-wheel steering system which comes into operation at high speed. Such precise suspension also required an extremely stiff bodyshell and the 300ZX's is 20 percent stiffer than the previous ZX.

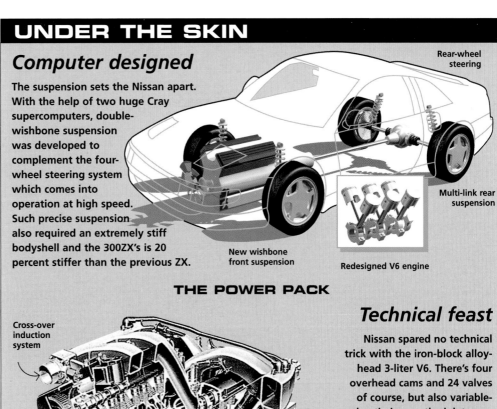

Rear-wheel steering

Multi-link rear suspension

New wishbone front suspension

Redesigned V6 engine

THE POWER PACK

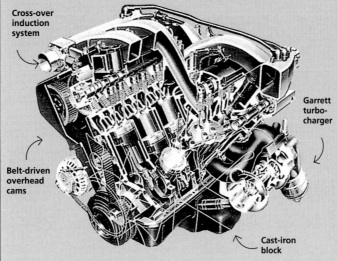

Cross-over induction system

Belt-driven overhead cams

Garrett turbo-charger

Cast-iron block

Technical feast

Nissan spared no technical trick with the iron-block alloy-head 3-liter V6. There's four overhead cams and 24 valves of course, but also variable-valve timing on the inlet cams and direct ignition with a separate coil for each spark plug. Two hybrid Garrett T2/T25 turbochargers are used, one for each bank of cylinders blowing through twin air-to-air intercoolers. For engine tuning, the induction pipes from each turbo are very long, each running across the engine.

Less is more

The pick of the bunch for the real enthusiast is the two-seater. It's shorter by around 15 inches, so it's lighter and, with a 5-inch shorter wheelbase, even more agile. Better still is the two-seater convertible available in 1992; Nissan's first fully open Z car.

Shorter wheelbase makes the two-seater more compact and desirable.

Nissan 300ZX TURBO

In 1990, the 300ZX was the most advanced and complicated sports car Nissan had ever built. It was gimmicky, but all the advanced technology was there for a good reason—to enable it to compete on equal terms with the best in the world.

Quad-cam V6

The V6 engine is a redesign of the V6 used in the previous 300ZX, with four cams and four valves per cylinder plus variable-valve timing. A 222-bhp normally aspirated version was available as well as the powerful turbo.

Twin turbos

Twin turbochargers give a quicker response than a single larger turbo does and they also reduce turbo lag.

Multi-link front suspension

The 300ZX's variation on front wishbone suspension is a curious design, with the upper arms almost level with the top of the coil springs, and actually projecting out over the top of each wheel.

Multi-link rear suspension

Not only does a multi-link system give good wheel control on the 300ZX, it's designed to give a small amount of toe-in under both braking and acceleration to keep the car stable.

Four-wheel steering

Some four-wheel steering systems are designed to make the car more maneuverable at low speeds, for easy parking, for example. The 300ZX's was designed to operate only at high speeds to improve cornering and lane changing.

Removable roof panels

The 300ZX's sunroof does not slide in the conventional way—the panels are removed manually and then stowed in a vinyl pouch in the trunk.

Intercooler vents

The vents below the square spotlights feed air to the engine's two intercoolers. An oil cooler is also mounted to the front.

Direct ignition

Each of the six cylinders has a spark plug with its own coil. Signals from the crankshaft-angle sensor determine when each coil fires. It's an absolutely precise system.

Flush-fitting glass

Nissan followed Audi's lead in equipping the 300ZX with flush-fitting side glass which looks more stylish and is also more aerodynamically efficient.

Specifications
1990 Nissan 300ZX Turbo

ENGINE

Type: V6
Construction: Cast-iron block and alloy cylinder heads
Valve gear: Four valves per cylinder operated by four overhead camshafts; variable timing on inlet cams
Bore and stroke: 3.4 in. x 3.3 in.
Displacement: 2,960 cc
Compression ratio: 8.5:1
Induction system: Electronic fuel injection with twin Garrett T2/25 intercooled turbochargers
Maximum power: 300 bhp at 6,400 rpm
Maximum torque: 273 lb-ft at 3,600 rpm

TRANSMISSION

Five-speed manual

BODY/CHASSIS

Steel monocoque with two-door coupe, two-seater or 2+2 body

SPECIAL FEATURES

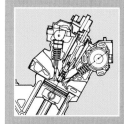

Twin cams on each bank of cylinders operate angled valves, with variable intake timing. Only one bank of cylinders is shown here.

Nissan's headlight supplier, Ichiko Kogyo, made a new glass pressing process for body-contoured headlights.

RUNNING GEAR

Steering: Rack-and-pinion
Front suspension: Multi-link with lower wishbones, coil springs, telescopic shocks and anti-roll bar
Rear suspension: Multi-link with coil springs, shocks and anti-roll bar
Brakes: Vented discs with ABS
Wheels: Cast-alloy 16 in.
Tires: 225/50 ZR16 (front), 245/45 ZR16 (rear)

DIMENSIONS

Length: 178.2 in.   **Width:** 70.9 in.
Height: 49.4 in.   **Wheelbase:** 101.2 in.
Track: 58.9 in. (front), 60.4 in. (rear)
Weight: 3,485 lbs.

Nissan SKYLINE GT-R

The Skyline may be Nissan's oldest nameplate, dating back to 1955, but the GT-R is part of the modern supercar era. An ultra-high-performance machine crammed with high technology, it is one of the fastest four seaters in the world.

"...maximum boosted power"

"It may have a huge rear spoiler and fat alloy wheels but, otherwise, the two-door GT-R doesn't look that special. Underneath, however, Nissan has created one of the most memorable driving machines ever. Keep the revs up to maintain maximum boosted power to enjoy all the performance you'll need. The steering is full of feel and the huge brakes are massively powerful. This is one of the world's quickest cars on winding roads."

The Skyline boasts a functional interior with excellent contoured bucket seats.

Milestones

1989 The first Skyline GT-R is unveiled as an ultra-high-performance version of the new, smoother-looking eighth-generation Skyline model.

The last real high performance sports car that Nissan made was the 300ZX.

1994 A new ninth-generation Skyline is launched, together with an improved GT-R V-Spec model. The car is sold in only right-hand-drive Far Eastern markets — mainly Japan and Australia.

The next fastest car in the current Nissan line-up is the 200SX.

1997 Having astounded the motoring press the world over, the GT-R makes its debut on the British market. As a very limited volume model just 100 are available in the first year. It becomes the quickest production car to lap the famous 14-mile Nürburgring circuit.

UNDER THE SKIN

High technology

Underneath, the Skyline GT-R is a haven of technological excellence. The shell itself is stiffened with tie-bars in the engine bay and trunk. State-of-the-art multi-link suspension provides excellent handling, and traction is aided by a split-torque system to the front and rear wheels. An active rear-wheel steer set-up eliminates understeer, and braking is provided by large-diameter vented discs.

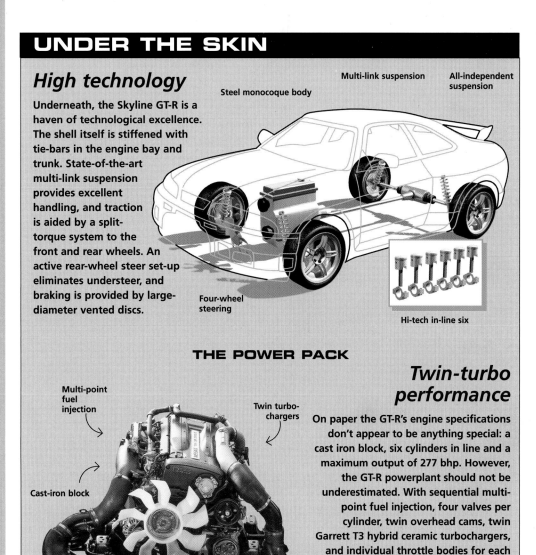

Steel monocoque body — Multi-link suspension — All-independent suspension

Four-wheel steering

Hi-tech in-line six

THE POWER PACK

Multi-point fuel injection

Twin turbo-chargers

Cast-iron block

Twin-turbo performance

On paper the GT-R's engine specifications don't appear to be anything special: a cast iron block, six cylinders in line and a maximum output of 277 bhp. However, the GT-R powerplant should not be underestimated. With sequential multi-point fuel injection, four valves per cylinder, twin overhead cams, twin Garrett T3 hybrid ceramic turbochargers, and individual throttle bodies for each cylinder, it wouldn't be out of place competing on the racetrack. The GT-R's power output can easily be boosted to nearly 500 bhp.

Awesome

The GT-R is an awesome machine in any form. It is offered as a two-door coupe or limited edition four-door sedan. For even more exclusivity and much more power, try the Autech-modified version, developed by Nissan's performance car division.

The GT-R offers outrageous performance by any standards.

Nissan SKYLINE GT-R

This car holds the record for the fastest lap by a production car at the famous Nürburgring circuit in Germany. The GT-R is a true performance machine for the keenest drivers.

Highly-tunable engine

The in-line six-cylinder engine is capable of delivering much more than it does in standard tune, since the GT-R's top speed is limited electronically to 135 mph. Most owners upgrade the engine's electronic management system to yield an extra 80 bhp.

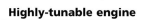

Active limited-slip differential

To prevent the rear tires from scrabbling under heavy acceleration, sensors on each rear wheel detect tire slip and automatically transfer more power to another wheel. Each wheel has its own multi-plate clutch so that the torque is infinitely variable between the wheels. Computer adjustments are made every 100th of a second.

Torque-split four-wheel drive

A computer-controlled four-wheel drive system provides optimum traction. Normally, 100 percent of drive is directed to the rear axle. Sensors analyze the car's traction and stability every 100th of a second. Up to 50 percent of the engine's torque can be directed to the front wheels.

Four-wheel steering

The Super HICAS four-wheel steering system has multiple sensors which detect steering input, turning rate, the car's speed, its yaw rate, and the lateral g-forces. It then calculates the amount of rear-wheel steer to be applied via an electric motor.

Adjustable rear spoiler

The body-colored rear spoiler mounted on the trunk lid is adjustable. It forms part of the GT-R body package, which also includes flared wheel arches, side skirts, an inset mesh grill and a deep front bumper/air dam.

Racing brakes

Behind the double five-spoke alloy wheels are very large vented disc brakes. They are 12.8 inch across at the front (with four-piston calipers made by Italian racing brake manufacturer Brembo). There is also a four-channel ABS anti-lock braking system.

Simple interior

The cockpit reflects the fact that the GT-R is based on a fairly standard sedan. Its plain black trim is only alleviated by attractive seats, carbon-fiber trim and alluring GT-R graphics.

Specifications

1998 Nissan Skyline GT-R

ENGINE

Type: In-line six-cylinder

Construction: Cast-iron cylinder block and aluminum cylinder head

Valve gear: Four valves per cylinder operated by double overhead camshafts

Bore and stroke: 3.38 in. x 2.91 in.

Displacement: 2,568 cc

Compression ratio: 8.5:1

Induction system: Sequential multi-point fuel injection

Maximum power: 277 bhp at 6,800 rpm

Maximum torque: 271 lb-ft at 4,400 rpm

TRANSMISSION

Five-speed manual

BODY/CHASSIS

Integral with two-door steel and aluminum coupe body

SPECIAL FEATURES

The rear spoiler is adjustable for rake to give varying amounts of down force.

Ferrari-style circular tail lights evoke a thoroughbred, racing flavor.

RUNNING GEAR

Steering: Rack-and-pinion

Front suspension: Multi-link with coil springs, telescopic shocks, and anti-roll bar

Rear suspension: Multi-link with coil springs telescopic shocks, and anti-roll bar

Brakes: Vented discs, 12.8-in. dia. (front), 11.8-in. dia. (rear)

Wheels: Alloy, 17-in. dia.

Tires: 245/45 ZR17

DIMENSIONS

Length: 184 in.   **Width:** 70.1 in.

Height: 53.5 in.   **Wheelbase:** 107.1 in.

Track: 58.3 in. (front), 57.9 in. (rear)

Weight: 3,530 lbs.

Panther SOLO

Panther aimed high with the Solo. It had the most advanced race car technology in its chassis, a mid-mounted engine and four-wheel drive. But the Solo could not be built at a cost people would pay and just 26 were made.

"...promises and delivers."

"With its wonderful instrument panel, complete with a huge central tachometer, the Solo promises a great deal. The combination of a mid-mounted, turbocharged twin-cam four and four-wheel drive results in tremendous cornering and very quick lap times, despite the relatively small tires. The steering is direct and responsive. Although the Solo has superb grip, its ride is very smooth for a supercar. The engine, however, suffers from turbo lag."

The Solo's businesslike cockpit is dominated by black-on-white gauges.

Milestones

1984 As the date approaches for the first Panther Solo to go into production, Toyota brings out the first MR2. Panther test-drives the MR2 and realizes the Solo cannot compete; the project is halted.

The Panther Solo uses the same turbocharged engine as Ford's Sierra RS Cosworth 4x4.

1989 After a long delay caused by the complexity of the new design—particularly the chassis—the Solo goes on sale late in the year, now with four-wheel drive. More than four years have elapsed since the press first sampled the Solo prototype.

The retro-style Panther Kallista is powered by Ford engines.

1990 After only 26 cars have been completed, Panther accepts defeat. The Solo is too expensive and build quality is not in the same league as rival supercars.

UNDER THE SKIN

Extreme complexity

Like a racing car, the Solo features a central survival cell which is both strong and light. It is built from composite materials—a mix of carbon fiber, fiberglass and Kevlar. At both ends of this cell are strong tubular steel subframes to carry the engine and running gear. The Cosworth twin-cam is mounted longitudinally, with drive going to all four wheels.

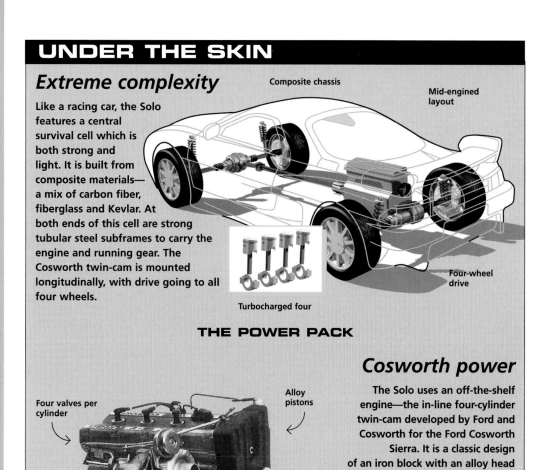

Composite chassis

Mid-engined layout

Four-wheel drive

Turbocharged four

THE POWER PACK

Four valves per cylinder

Alloy pistons

Cast-iron block with alloy head

Turbocharged and intercooled

Cosworth power

The Solo uses an off-the-shelf engine—the in-line four-cylinder twin-cam developed by Ford and Cosworth for the Ford Cosworth Sierra. It is a classic design of an iron block with an alloy head holding two belt-driven camshafts. These operate 16 valves, at an angle of 45 degrees, in hemispherical combustion chambers. The valves are large because the engine is oversquare with a large bore and short stroke. Like many performance cars of the era, the Solo relies on a Garrett turbocharger to boost power.

Original Solo

The earlier Solo was a simpler model. Although mid-engined, it was only two-wheel drive. Unlike the production car, it had a traditional steel chassis, clothed with fiberglass bodywork. Power came from the Cosworth four-cylinder turbo engine.

The later Solos were more high-tech than the original.

Panther SOLO

In theory it was a winner—a true four-wheel drive supercar to rival the best. In practice, however, its late introduction, high price and poor build quality deterred many would-be buyers.

Composite construction

The Solo's construction was complicated and was very expensive to manufacture. It has steel subframes front and rear, with the body composed of a mix of composite and fiberglass panels.

Intercooler air intake

The intercooler for the turbocharger is mounted at the back of the engine compartment under the rear spoiler.

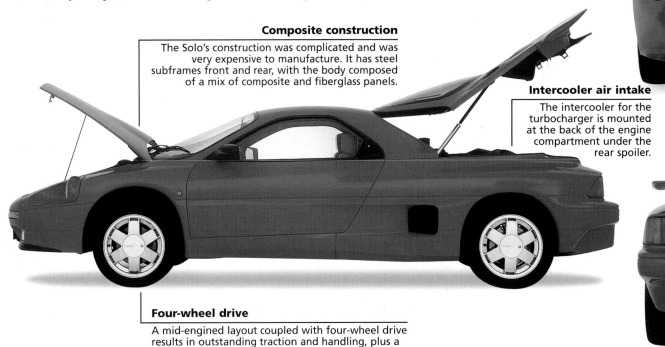

Four-wheel drive

A mid-engined layout coupled with four-wheel drive results in outstanding traction and handling, plus a drivetrain layout that is unique among supercars.

Functional rear spoiler

Wind tunnel testing produced the correct wing profile and angle to give rear downforce. The rear wing is complemented by the action of the car's underbody that helps to suck the rear of the car to the road.

Wishbone suspension
Double unequal length wishbones are used front and rear, although they are offset to clear the driveshafts.

Specifications

1989 Panther Solo

ENGINE
Type: Ford Cosworth in-line four

Construction: Cast-iron block and alloy head

Valve gear: Four valves per cylinder operated by twin belt-driven overhead camshafts

Bore and stroke: 3.57 in. x 3.03 in.

Displacement: 1,993 cc

Compression ratio: 8.0:1

Induction system: Weber-Marelli electronic fuel injection with intercooled Garrett T3B turbocharger

Maximum power: 204 bhp at 6,000 rpm

Maximum torque: 198 lb-ft at 4,500 rpm

TRANSMISSION
Five-speed manual with four-wheel drive and center and rear viscous couplings

BODY/CHASSIS
Steel floorpan and front and rear subframes with composite central cell and bodywork

SPECIAL FEATURES

Large scoops behind the rear window feed air to the radiator.

Instead of pop-up units, pods revolve to reveal the lights.

RUNNING GEAR
Steering: Rack-and-pinion

Front suspension: MacPherson struts with lower wishbones

Rear suspension: Double wishbones with coil springs and Bilstein shock absorbers

Brakes: Vented discs, 10.24-in. dia (front), 10.75-in. dia (rear); ABS standard

Wheels: Alloy, 6 x 15 in.

Tires: Goodyear Eagles NCT, 195/50 VR15 (front), 205/50 VR15 (rear)

DIMENSIONS
Length: 171.0 in.   **Width:** 71.0 in.

Height: 46.4 in.   **Wheelbase:** 99.6 in.

Track: 60.2 in. (front), 59.6 in. (rear)

Weight: 2,723 lbs.

Porsche 993 TURBO

Porsche's 993 was the last of the 911 Turbo line to have the famous air-cooled flat-six engine. In this case it was a 3.6-liter producing more than 400 bhp, enough to give 180-mph performance. Roadholding was staggering, too.

"...fantastic grip."

"Twin turbos give simply awesome performance. Row through the six gears and the 993 can hit 100 mph in 9.3 seconds—its passing power is breathtaking. Porsche decided it wanted a car with the greatest possible roadholding so the four-wheel drive gives fantastic grip through wide tires. It feels impossible to drift the car; no matter how fast you corner, your bravery runs out long before the car loses grip."

The fascia of the 993 has a clean and solid look to it.

Milestones

1975 The first 911 Turbo
is released. The 930 has a single large KKK turbo and produces 245 bhp from 3 liters, to give a top speed of 150 mph with 0-60 in 6.1 seconds.

The Group B racing 959 was the first four-wheel drive Porsche.

1991 After a two-year
gap in production, the second-generation Turbo appears, with a larger turbocharger giving 315 bhp. As well as the two-wheel drive car, the four-wheel drive Carrera 4 is available.

The 993 has smoother lines than the preceding 911s.

1995 The third generation
Turbo is launched. It has a double-wishbone rear suspension and four-wheel drive. Power climbs to 400 bhp thanks to the use of two intercooled turbochargers.

UNDER THE SKIN

Four-wheel drive

Like the rest of the 911 family, the 993 Turbo has its engine mounted at the rear, beyond the rear-axle line. It has a refined four-wheel drive variable-split system with center viscous coupling. Rear suspension is a double-wishbone setup and the front has a modified MacPherson strut system, introduced on the first Carrera 4 in 1989. There is power-assisted rack-and-pinion steering, and the brakes are enormous vented discs.

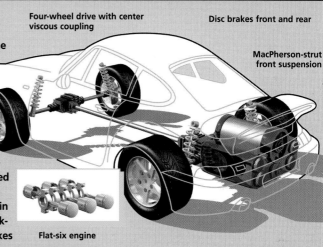

Four-wheel drive with center viscous coupling

Disc brakes front and rear

MacPherson-strut front suspension

Flat-six engine

THE POWER PACK

Hard-hitting boxer

By the end of the 1980s, Porsche's famous flat-six boxer engine had been increased to 3.6 liters for the first Carrera 4. In order to do so, it needed a new block, which was to be carried over for use in the 1993 Turbo. It was very oversquare at 4.00 inches x 3.05 inches, with a very wide bore, but there were still only two large valves per cylinder opened by just one overhead camshaft per bank. The key to its power output was one intercooled KKK turbocharger per bank of cylinders. With simple modifications it could produce up to 450 bhp in a road spec car.

Turbo S

Beyond the standard 993 Turbo was the winged Turbo S, with big air intakes in the rear wheel arches. This has power boosted up to 424 bhp at 5,750 rpm, along with 400 lb-ft of torque. Sensational acceleration and 180 mph were easily attainable.

The Porsche 993 has refined road manners and staggering performance.

Porsche **993 TURBO**

Wide and low, with huge flared rear wheel arches and distinctive sloping headlamps, the 993 Turbo is still instantly recognizable as a descendant of the very first 911 from the early 1960s.

Twin turbos

The flat-six-engine design lent itself to having one turbocharger for each bank of cylinders. Porsche used small German-made KKK K-16 turbos. Each one could thus be placed as close as possible to an exhaust manifold, quickening its response time and virtually eliminating lag.

Integrated bumpers

At the same time that Porsche changed the front headlamp design, it merged the bodywork and bumpers together into one smooth shape.

Alloy wheels

Alloy wheels have long been fitted to Porsche Turbos—they just keep getting bigger and bigger. Turbo 993s have massive 18-inch diameter alloys. They are this large for a couple of reasons: to accommodate brake discs that are greater than a foot in diameter and to carry very wide low-profile tires.

Four-wheel drive

Porsche applied four-wheel drive to the Carrera 4 in 1989 and then modified it for the second-generation model, with a wider variable torque split. It was this system, with its center viscous coupling and rear limited-slip differential that is applied to the 993 Turbo. Drive would normally be automatically applied to the rear wheels until the car's sensors detect that torque needs to be fed to the front wheels as well.

Rear-heavy

Despite being four-wheel drive and having the additional weight of two front drive-shafts, extended propshaft and front differential, the weight distribution of the 993 Turbo is still heavily rear-biased, with 55 percent of the weight at the back.

Specifications

1997 Porsche 993 Turbo

ENGINE

Type: Flat six

Construction: Alloy block and heads

Valve gear: Two valves per cylinder operated by a single overhead cam per bank of cylinders

Bore and stroke: 4.0 in. x 3.05 in.

Displacement: 3,600 cc

Compression ratio: 8.0:1

Induction system: Bosch electronic fuel injection with twin KKK turbochargers

Maximum power: 400 bhp at 5,750 rpm

Max torque: 400 lb-ft at 4,500 rpm

TRANSMISSION

Six-speed manual with permanent four-wheel drive

BODY/CHASSIS

Unitary monocoque construction with steel two-door coupe body

SPECIAL FEATURES

The large alloy wheels house the massive vented disc brakes.

The huge rear spoiler produces downforce and aids straight-line stability.

RUNNING GEAR

Steering: Rack-and-pinion

Front suspension: MacPherson struts with lower wishbones and anti-roll bar

Rear suspension: Double wishbones with coil springs, telescopic shock absorbers and anti-roll bar

Brakes: Vented discs, 12.7-in. dia. (front and rear)

Wheels: Cast alloy, 8 in. x 18 in. (front), 10 in. x 18 in. rear

Tires: 225/40 ZR18 (front), 285/30 ZR18 (rear)

DIMENSIONS

Length: 167.7 in. **Width:** 70.7 in.

Height: 51.8 in. **Wheelbase:** 89.4 in.

Track: 55.5 in. (front), 59.3 in. (rear)

Weight: 3,307 lbs.

Shelby **CSX**

With the CSX, Carroll Shelby showed that you could take an ordinary four-cylinder front-drive car such as the Dodge Shadow and turn it into a high-performance, 130-mph-plus sports coupe.

"...impressive power."

"When using all the 175 bhp from a standstill you better hang on because the torque-steer will nearly wrench the steering wheel out of your hands. Slightly ease off the throttle and control will return. With the optional bigger tires, the car fidgets and darts. The ride is very firm, and the payoff is a decent level of grip and handling that lets you use all the engine's power. Because the turbo lag is minimal, there is always plenty of passing power."

The interior of the CSX has a bland, functional look to it.

Milestones

1987 Carroll Shelby
turns his attention to the Dodge Shadow compact. He modifies the suspension and adds a Garrett turbocharger.

Carroll Shelby tuned many Chrysler Corp. products during the 1980s.

1989 A limited
edition (just 500 cars), with improved interior, lowered and stiffened suspension, rear wing and front air dam, optional larger tires and a new variable intake turbocharger, is launched. It marks the debut of composite fiberglass road wheels.

The Dodge Neon R/T is the spiritual successor to the CSX.

1990 Chrysler builds
its own turbocharged version of the Shadow after Shelby stops making the CSX.

1991 The final year
of the Shadow sees a reduction in power, even from the 2.2-liter turbo, which pumps out a mere 150 bhp.

UNDER THE SKIN

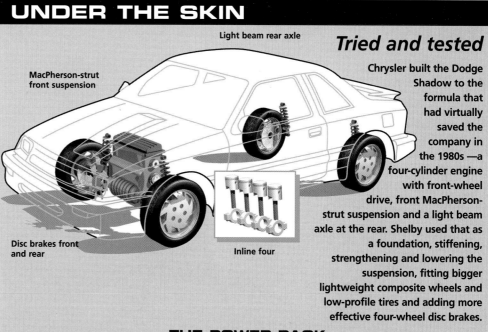

Light beam rear axle

MacPherson-strut front suspension

Disc brakes front and rear

Inline four

Tried and tested

Chrysler built the Dodge Shadow to the formula that had virtually saved the company in the 1980s —a four-cylinder engine with front-wheel drive, front MacPherson-strut suspension and a light beam axle at the rear. Shelby used that as a foundation, stiffening, strengthening and lowering the suspension, fitting bigger lightweight composite wheels and low-profile tires and adding more effective four-wheel disc brakes.

THE POWER PACK

VNT power

Chrysler's familiar overhead-cam, four-cylinder dates back to the early 1980s. It has a cast-iron block with a crankshaft running on five main bearings and topped by an alloy head with a single beltdriven overhead camshaft and two valves per cylinder operated by hydraulic valve lifters. It is undersquare, with a stroke longer than the bore is wide (3.44 inches x 3.62 inches), giving just over 2.2 liters. At first, power output was very low, but the addition of Chrysler's new Variable Nozzle Turbocharger (VNT) not only raised power to 175 bhp, but also considerably reduced turbolag.

My generation

A second-generation CSX model has to be the one to go for because there were so many improvements over the original. This is especially the case in terms of power delivery, if not outright power, as well as suspension improvements and superior handling.

The understated looks of the CSX belie its performance potential.

Shelby CSX

The standard Dodge Shadow was not an outstanding-looking car, and Shelby had to dress it up to look the part. This involved lowering it, fitting low-profile tires and adding a full bodykit with front spoiler and rear wing.

Power-assisted steering

A nose-heavy car with front-drive and wide low-profile tires is always going to need power assistance for the rack-and-pinion steering. The steering is also very high-geared, with just 2.1 turns lock to lock, making the car very responsive to driver input.

Overhead-cam engine

Chrysler's overhead-cam four-cylinder engine had been designed with turbocharging in mind and, with the compression ratio dropped to 8.1:1, it was strong enough to take the 12-psi of turbo boost from the VNT turbo.

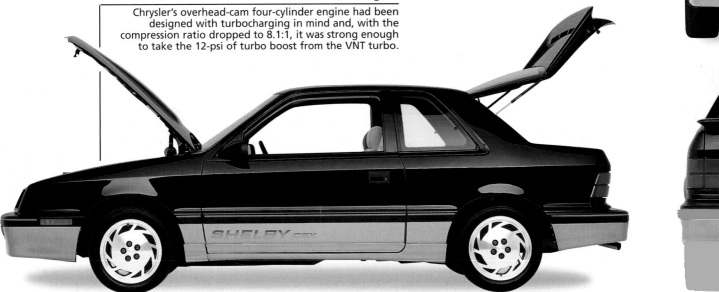

High front weight bias

Having the iron-block engine mounted transversely at the front with its transmission and turbo makes the CSX front-heavy. The weight distribution is 62:38 front/rear, which would normally create excessive understeer, yet Shelby was able to minimize this.

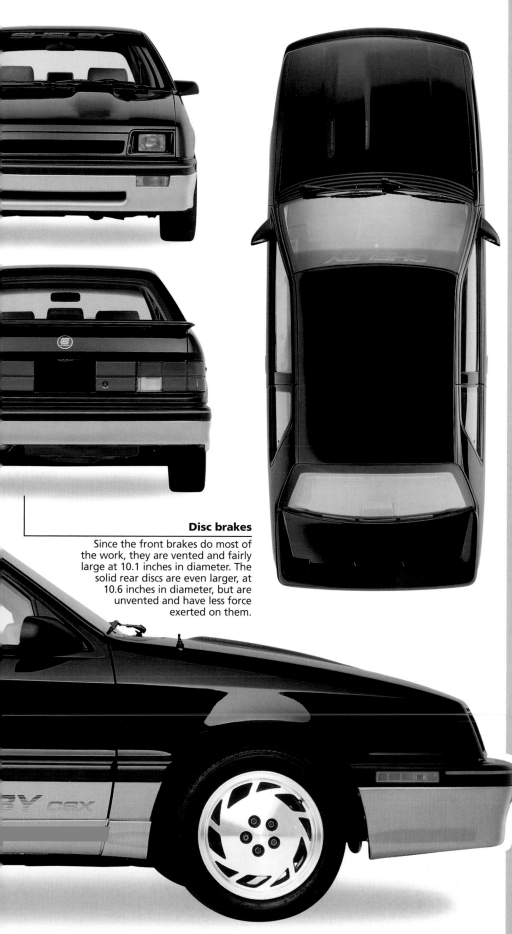

Disc brakes

Since the front brakes do most of the work, they are vented and fairly large at 10.1 inches in diameter. The solid rear discs are even larger, at 10.6 inches in diameter, but are unvented and have less force exerted on them.

Specifications

1989 Shelby CSX

ENGINE

Type: Inline four-cylinder

Construction: Cast-iron block and alloy cylinder head

Valve gear: Two valves per cylinder operated by a single beltdriven overhead camshaft

Bore and stroke: 3.5 in. x 3.68 in.

Displacement: 2,213 cc

Compression ratio: 8.1:1

Induction system: Electronic fuel injection with Garrett AiResearch VNT-25 turbo

Maximum power: 175 bhp at 5,200 rpm

Maximum torque: 205 lb-ft at 2,400 rpm

TRANSMISSION

Five-speed manual

BODY/CHASSIS

Unitary steel construction

SPECIAL FEATURES

With a top speed of over 130 mph, the CSX needed its rear wing to keep it stable at high speeds.

The turbo boost gauge is the only real indication of what lurks under the hood.

RUNNING GEAR

Steering: Rack-and-pinion

Front suspension: MacPherson struts with lower control arms and anti-roll bar

Rear suspension: Beam axle with trailing arms, Panhard rod, coil springs, telescopic shock absorbers and anti-roll bar

Brakes: Vented discs, 10.1-in. dia. (front), solid discs, 10.6-in. dia. (rear)

Wheels: Plastic fiberglass-reinforced composite, 15 x 6.5 in.

Tires: 225/50 VR15

DIMENSIONS

Length: 171.7 in.

Width: 67.3 in.

Height: 52.0 in.

Wheelbase: 97.0 in.

Track: 57.6 in. (front and rear)

Weight: 2,790 lbs.

Toyota SUPRA

With the 1993 model, Toyota moved the Supra from an overweight and ugly cruiser to an affordable and dramatically styled junior supercar capable of more than 155 mph thanks to its 326-bhp twin-turbo, twin-cam engine.

"...Be prepared for excitement."

"On looks alone, the Supra has a very extroverted styling. When you slide behind the wheel and stomp the accelerator to the floor, be prepared for excitement. Off idle, the whistling under the hood indicates that the first turbocharger is spooling up. At 4,000 rpm both turbos are now forcing air into the Supra's 2,997 cc engine. The engine is tuned for mid- to high-end power, but because of a governor, can only get the car up to 156 mph. Without it the Supra would easily hit 180 mph."

The luxurious interior of the twin-turbo Supra really gave Nissan, Mazda and Porsche something to worry about.

Milestones

1984 The six-cylinder
Supra line begins with a 2.8-liter car with the crisp, sharp-edged styling similar to that used on the contemporary Celica. The car is normally aspirated and not very impressive. The Supra reaches 60 mph in 7.9 seconds and has a top speed of 125 mph.

The Supra was the first Toyota six-cylinder sports car since the exotic 2000GT.

1986 Supra gets a
facelift with a much more rounded shape and a power output increased to 201 bhp, giving a top speed of 135 mph.

The second-generation Supra was fast, but not as competent as the current model.

1989 Hinting at the
way Toyota was going to go, the Supra is given more power with a turbocharged version of the straight-six engine that produces 232 bhp.

1993 The current
Supra is introduced two years later than planned. Extra time was needed to build a car to outperform the Nissan 300ZX. It is more powerful, lighter and faster than the previous model.

UNDER THE SKIN

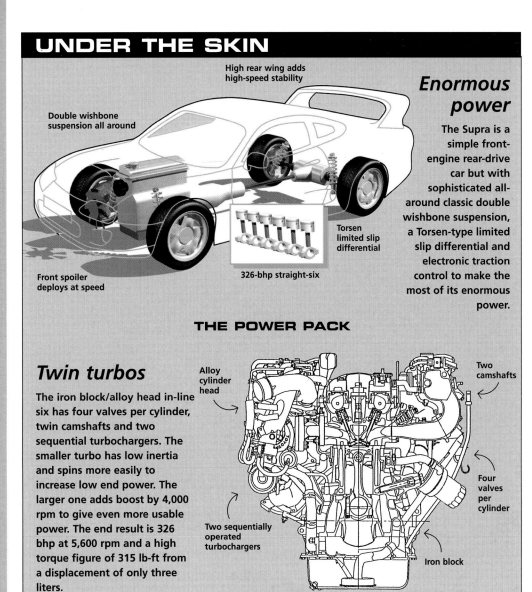

High rear wing adds high-speed stability

Double wishbone suspension all around

Front spoiler deploys at speed

Torsen limited slip differential

326-bhp straight-six

Enormous power

The Supra is a simple front-engine rear-drive car but with sophisticated all-around classic double wishbone suspension, a Torsen-type limited slip differential and electronic traction control to make the most of its enormous power.

THE POWER PACK

Twin turbos

The iron block/alloy head in-line six has four valves per cylinder, twin camshafts and two sequential turbochargers. The smaller turbo has low inertia and spins more easily to increase low end power. The larger one adds boost by 4,000 rpm to give even more usable power. The end result is 326 bhp at 5,600 rpm and a high torque figure of 315 lb-ft from a displacement of only three liters.

Alloy cylinder head

Two camshafts

Four valves per cylinder

Two sequentially operated turbochargers

Iron block

Flashy and fast

Some critics find the Supra too flashy, but they should take another look beyond the tall wing and massive hood and side scoops. It's hard to fault the Supra's lines, as it looks good from any angle and it is given real presence by those large-diameter wheels.

The flashy Supra has all the power to match its extraordinary looks.

Toyota SUPRA

The previous Supra was quick but bland, clumsy looking and clumsy to drive—the current sports car, however, is in another class. Stunning looks and that high rear wing promise high performance, and that's exactly what the Supra delivers.

Traction control

Using the ABS sensors, traction control works by lightly applying the rear brakes, reducing fuel supply and retarding ignition just enough to stop the rear wheels from spinning.

Six-speed transmission

Like the Porsche 968, the Supra uses the tough Getrag six-speed transmission. However, the turbocharged engine isn't peaky and does not need constant gear shifting to get the best from it.

Tall rear wing

The huge wing helps the Supra remain stable at the high speeds it can easily reach.

G-sensing ABS

The Supra ABS anti-lock braking system has a *g*-force sensor so the brakes are modulated through corners to stop the brakes from locking and the car sliding.

Extending front spoiler

If the Supra travels above 56 mph for more than five seconds, the front spoiler automatically deploys to increase front downforce.

Twin wishbone suspension

Classic racing-style double-wishbone suspension is used in the front and rear to give excellent wheel location and precise handling.

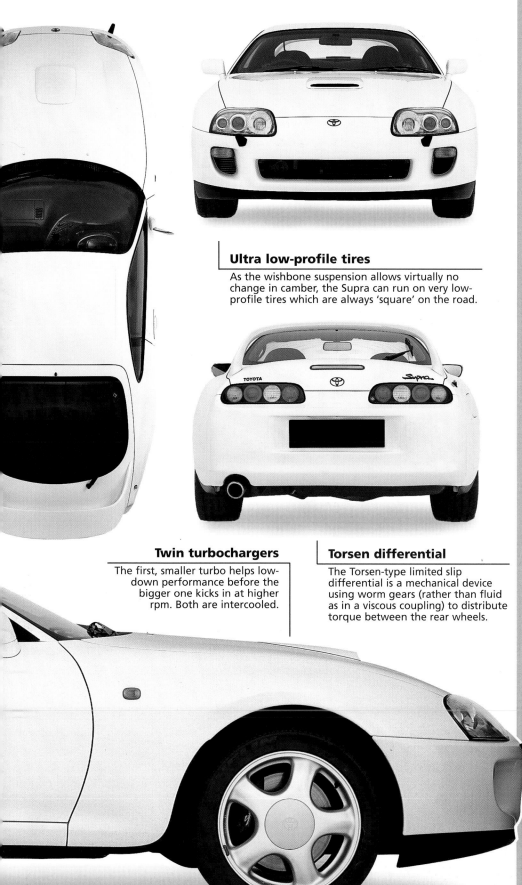

Specifications
1996 Toyota Supra

ENGINE

Type: Straight-six twin-cam
Construction: Cast-iron block and alloy cylinder head
Valve gear: Four valves per cylinder operated by twin overhead cams
Bore and stroke: 3.39 in. x 3.39 in.
Displacement: 2,997 cc
Induction system: Electronic fuel injection with twin sequential turbochargers
Maximum power: 326 bhp at 5,600 rpm
Maximum torque: 315 lb-ft at 4,800 rpm

TRANSMISSION

Six-speed manual or four-speed automatic

BODY/CHASSIS

Steel monocoque two-door 2+2 coupe

SPECIAL FEATURES

The Supra receives stability at high speeds thanks to this enormous wing.

Sequential turbos give the Supra its power—one operates at lower rpm for improved torque, the other comes on by 4,000 rpm for high-end power.

RUNNING GEAR

Steering: Rack-and-pinion
Front suspension: Twin wishbones with coil springs, telescopic shock absorbers and anti-roll bar
Rear suspension: Twin wishbones with coil springs, telescopic shock absorbers and anti-roll bar
Brakes: Four-wheel vented discs, 12.6 in. dia. with ABS
Wheels/tires: Alloy 8 in. x 17 in. (front), 9.5 in. x 17 in. (rear) with 235/45 ZR17 (front) and 255/40 ZR17 (rear) tires

DIMENSIONS

Length: 177.8 in.   **Width:** 71.3 in.
Wheelbase: 100.4 in.   **Height:** 49.8 in.
Track: 59.8 in. (front), 60 in. (rear)
Weight: 3,445 lbs.

Ultra low-profile tires
As the wishbone suspension allows virtually no change in camber, the Supra can run on very low-profile tires which are always 'square' on the road.

Twin turbochargers
The first, smaller turbo helps low-down performance before the bigger one kicks in at higher rpm. Both are intercooled.

Torsen differential
The Torsen-type limited slip differential is a mechanical device using worm gears (rather than fluid as in a viscous coupling) to distribute torque between the rear wheels.

171

TVR **CHIMAERA**

Although milder than the fearsome Griffith, the Chimaera is still a seriously fast sports car, built using the same recipe that makes early Corvettes great: a separate chassis, fiberglass body and a big V8 driving the rear wheels.

"...made for skillful drivers."

"Chimaeras are made for skillful drivers. There's a lot of power for a car with such a short wheelbase (14 inches shorter than a Corvette), and it's set up to give instant response to the incredibly quick steering. It's easily steered on the throttle, too. The V8 sounds great, and is accompanied by flexible power that gives serious overtaking ability. What's more, the ride is nowhere near as hard as you'd expect and the TVR feels immensely solid."

Classy gauges and a chunky wheel hint at the Chimaera's potent performance.

Milestones

1993 TVR launches the Chimaera, which fills a hole in its range between the popular 'S' convertible and the mighty 5.0-liter Griffith.

The Griffith was the first of the modern wave of TVRs.

1995 At the top of the Chimaera range

now is the 5.0-liter version with the bored and stroked Rover engine from the Griffith 500, giving 340 bhp.

The Cerbera currently tops the TVR range.

1997 TVR fills a gap between the 240-bhp 4.0-liter and 340-bhp 5.0-liter with the 4.5-liter version. The new engine is a long-stroke version of the 4.0-liter and gives 285 bhp at 5,500 rpm and 310 lb-ft of torque at 4,250 rpm. It has the same improvements as the 5.0-liter car, so there are bigger brakes, and new wheels that carry the Bridgestone S-02 tires are now fitted to all TVRs.

UNDER THE SKIN

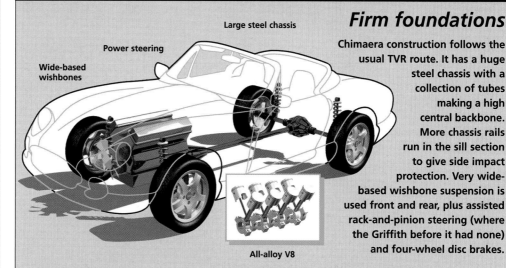

Power steering · Large steel chassis · Wide-based wishbones · All-alloy V8

Firm foundations

Chimaera construction follows the usual TVR route. It has a huge steel chassis with a collection of tubes making a high central backbone. More chassis rails run in the sill section to give side impact protection. Very wide-based wishbone suspension is used front and rear, plus assisted rack-and-pinion steering (where the Griffith before it had none) and four-wheel disc brakes.

THE POWER PACK

GM development

Although TVR now has its own V8 engine design, the V8s used in the Chimaera are developments of the old all-alloy ex-Buick V8 sold to Rover. The engine is a simple design with a single V-mounted camshaft, push-rods, rockers and hydraulic lifters to actuate two valves per cylinder. Rover stretched it from 3.5 to 4.0 liters by increasing the bore in the alloy block, but in the TVR installation the compression ratio is increased to a high 9.8:1 and power to 240 bhp.

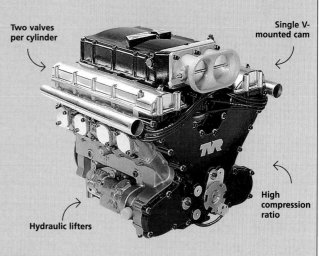

Two valves per cylinder · Single V-mounted cam · High compression ratio · Hydraulic lifters

Top choice

The ultimate Chimaera is the 5.0-liter, which has the biggest stretch of the old Rover engine. It takes power up to 340 bhp and torque to 320 lb-ft. Naturally, performance rockets too, with a top speed of 165 mph and a 0-60 time of 4.1 seconds.

The 5.0-liter Chimaera is an exclusive beast that should be handled with care.

TVR CHIMAERA

Stunning looks as well as performance set the Chimaera apart. TVR styling is all carried out in-house in Blackpool, with traditional clay full-size models sculpted until the effect is just right.

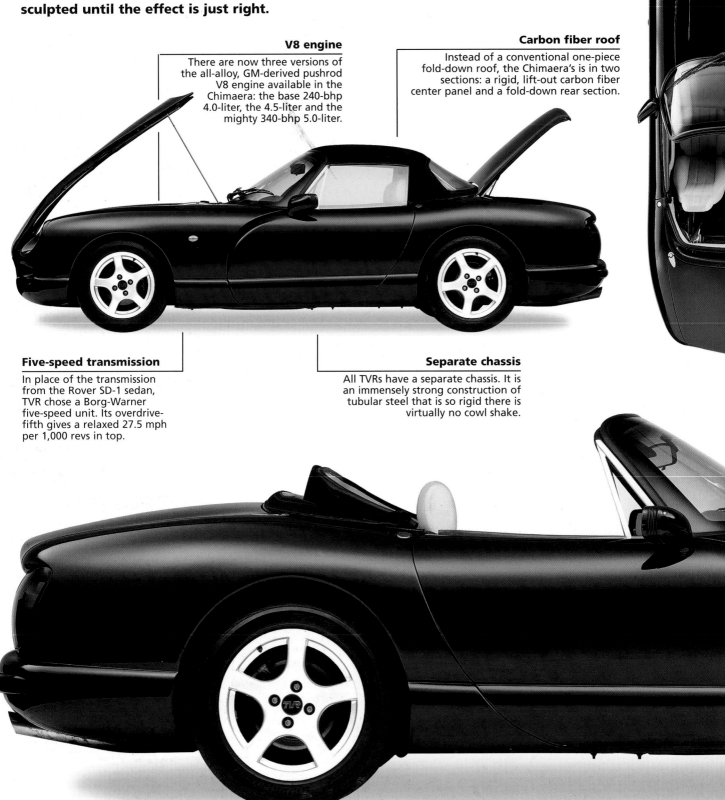

V8 engine
There are now three versions of the all-alloy, GM-derived pushrod V8 engine available in the Chimaera: the base 240-bhp 4.0-liter, the 4.5-liter and the mighty 340-bhp 5.0-liter.

Carbon fiber roof
Instead of a conventional one-piece fold-down roof, the Chimaera's is in two sections: a rigid, lift-out carbon fiber center panel and a fold-down rear section.

Five-speed transmission
In place of the transmission from the Rover SD-1 sedan, TVR chose a Borg-Warner five-speed unit. Its overdrive-fifth gives a relaxed 27.5 mph per 1,000 revs in top.

Separate chassis
All TVRs have a separate chassis. It is an immensely strong construction of tubular steel that is so rigid there is virtually no cowl shake.

Rack-and-pinion steering
Rack-and-pinion steering is almost universal in sports cars, but what sets the TVR's apart is the extreme quickness of the rack. It is very high-geared, with only 1.9 turns lock to lock, making the car highly controllable in a slide.

Equal weight distribution
Mounting the engine well back in the chassis results in 50/50 weight distribution front and rear. This, plus short front and rear overhangs, give the Chimaera excellent handling.

Specifications

1998 TVR Chimaera

ENGINE
Type: V8

Construction: Alloy block and heads

Valve gear: Two valves per cylinder operated by a single camshaft with pushrods and rocker arms

Bore and stroke: 3.70 in. x 2.80 in.

Displacement: 3,950 cc

Compression ratio: 9.8:1

Induction system: Electronic fuel injection

Maximum power: 240 bhp at 5,250 rpm

Maximum torque: 270 lb-ft at 4,000 rpm

TRANSMISSION
Five-speed manual

BODY/CHASSIS
Separate tubular-steel backbone chassis with fiberglass two-seater convertible body

SPECIAL FEATURES

The rear of the roof folds into the trunk, where the center section can be stored.

All TVRs are styled in-house at the company's Blackpool base.

RUNNING GEAR
Steering: Rack-and-pinion

Front suspension: Double wishbones with coil springs, telescopic shock absorbers and anti-roll bar

Rear suspension: Double wishbones with coil springs, telescopic shock absorbers and anti-roll bar

Brakes: Vented discs, 10.2-in. dia. (front), 10.7-in. dia. (rear)

Wheels: Cast-alloy, 7 x 15 in. (front), 7 x 16 in. (rear)

Tires: Bridgestone S-02, 205/60 ZR15 (front), 225/55 ZR16 (rear)

DIMENSIONS
Length: 179.1 in.   **Width:** 76.2 in.

Height: 50.2 in.   **Wheelbase:** 98.4 in.

Track: 57.5 in. (front and rear)

Weight: 2,260 lbs.

TVR **TUSCAN RACER**

"They're very frightening," was TVR chairman Peter Wheeler's comment about the Tuscan racers. With their monstrous performance, that was no understatement. The Tuscan Challenge quickly established itself as one of the fastest and most entertaining race series.

"...acceleration defies belief."

"The Tuscan has a reputation as the most brutal British race car due to its power, which is simply awesome. In such a light frame, acceleration defies belief. In the corners, you have to pick a perfect driving line or, as one racer commented, 'It tells you you've got things wrong by swapping ends several times.' The brakes are phenomenal, though it's best to stroke the pedal rather than stamp on it to avoid lock up."

The Tuscan's cabin maintains the feel of a road car but with an additional roll cage.

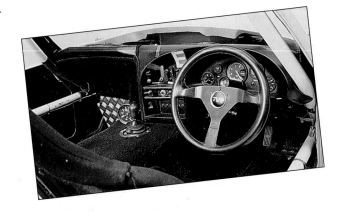

Milestones

1988 With the TVR 420 SEAC

banned from regular competition because it was much faster than any competitor on the track, TVR decides to launch its own one-make racing series. The TVR Tuscan Challenge is announced at the Birmingham Motor Show.

The first race-derived TVR Tuscan featured a Ford V8 engine.

1989 The first Tuscan

Challenge race takes place on May 7th at Donington Park. It was a huge success.

TVR developed the Griffith as a street-going counterpart of the more powerful Tuscan.

1999 Ten years after the first

series began, the Tuscan Challenge still continues with its popularity undiminished. It is successful because it is affordable, and since it requires identical cars the emphasis is placed on driver skill and stamina rather than mechanical prowess.

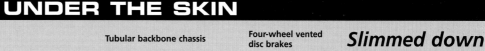

UNDER THE SKIN

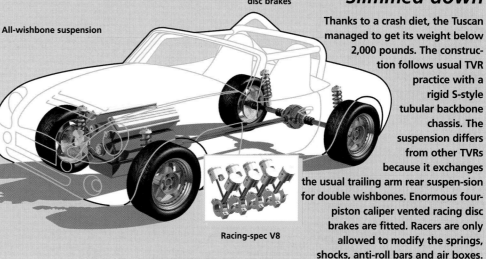

All-wishbone suspension

Tubular backbone chassis

Four-wheel vented disc brakes

Racing-spec V8

Slimmed down

Thanks to a crash diet, the Tuscan managed to get its weight below 2,000 pounds. The construction follows usual TVR practice with a rigid S-style tubular backbone chassis. The suspension differs from other TVRs because it exchanges the usual trailing arm rear suspen-sion for double wishbones. Enormous four-piston caliper vented racing disc brakes are fitted. Racers are only allowed to modify the springs, shocks, anti-roll bars and air boxes.

THE POWER PACK

Gargantuan Rover V8

Like all TVRs of the period, the Tuscan's engine is derived from the classic aluminum Rover 3.5 liter V8. It is a development of a Buick engine from 1961. The block and steel crankshaft comes from Rover. The rest of the internals are mostly made by TVR, with Carillo rods and four Dellorto downdraft carburetors. In the first season, the 4.4-liter engine was tuned to its maximum limit to produce 400 bhp at 7,000 rpm and 361 lb-ft of torque at 5,500 rpm. The result is a stunning 0–60 mph time of just 3.6 seconds and a top speed of 165 mph. The huge power made for close, exciting racing.

Entertainment

The Tuscan Challenge Race Series is still going strong, providing some of the best racing for drivers and spectators alike. Four owners have even done the unthinkable and converted one of the world's fastest racing cars into a roadgoing projectile.

With 400 bhp and relatively skinny tires, the Tuscan can be a handful.

TVR **TUSCAN RACER**

In the 1980s, TVR racing cars were faster than anything else in their class, so they were banned from racing. TVR's solution was to create an all-new, one-make racing series with a ferocious new car—the Tuscan.

Racing disc brakes

Massive 11.8-inch diameter vented disc brakes are fitted on all four wheels. Customers are not allowed to alter the discs themselves, although brake pad material, brake fluid, and master cylinder bores can be changed as desired.

V8 power

The basis of TVR's 4.4-liter V8 engine is the perennial Rover all-alloy unit, but TVR is a master at tuning this powerplant. By the time it had finished with this mill, the power output was in excess of 400 bhp.

Narrow tires

The Tuscan racers deliberately use small tires to make the racing more interesting. They are only 8.3 inches wide, on 9 x 16 inch OZ racing split-rim alloy wheels.

Lightweight chassis

The tubular backbone chassis is basically the same as the one used on TVR road cars. Its lightness helps keep the car's weight down. The regulations state that the car must weigh at least 1,764 lbs.

Fiberglass bodywork

The body panels are made from lightweight fiberglass and are not load bearing. It was originally intended to offer the Tuscan as a road car as well, but the cost of re-engineering the body persuaded TVR to develop an all-new street model called the Griffith.

Specifications

1989 TVR Tuscan Racer

ENGINE
Type: V8

Construction: Aluminum block and heads

Valve gear: Two valves per cylinder operated by a single chain-driven camshaft with pushrods and rockers

Bore and stroke: 3.70 in. x 3.15 in.

Displacement: 4,441 cc

Compression ratio: 12.85:1

Induction system: Four Dellorto 2V carburetors

Maximum power: 400 bhp at 7,000 rpm

Maximum torque: 361 lb-ft at 5,500 rpm

TRANSMISSION
Five-speed manual

BODY/CHASSIS
Separate tubular chassis with fiberglass two-door open body

SPECIAL FEATURES

The built-in roll-cage provides maximum rigidity and strength.

According to regulations, the cowled headlights are fully functional.

RUNNING GEAR
Steering: Rack-and-pinion

Front suspension: Double wishbones with coil springs, shock absorbers and anti-roll bar

Rear suspension: Double wishbones with coil springs, shock absorbers and anti-roll bar

Brakes: Discs (front and rear)

Wheels: Alloy, 16-in. dia.

Tires: 210/60 x 16

DIMENSIONS
Length: 155.0 in. **Width:** 68.5 in.

Height: 46.5 in. **Wheelbase:** 92.0 in.

Track: 58.3 in. (front and rear)

Weight: 1,765 lbs.

Ultima SPYDER

The only limit to the Ultima kit is your ambition. The brave and committed Chevy V8 makes the lightweight, mid-engined, race-car-inspired Mk IV faster than the current Corvette or Viper.

Ultima Spyder

"...enormous grip."

"Slither in and sit on the hard, racing bucket seats. Fire up the Chevy V8 and slide the rose-jointed shift lever into gear. The performance is simply staggering. It is said that one Ultima hit 100 mph in 6.8 seconds, and it's easy to believe. There's just no body roll, no play anywhere in the suspension and it has incredibly precise steering. The mid-engined layout eliminates under- and oversteer, while the enormous grip is just about unbreakable."

There are few creature comforts in the Ultima Spyder, just the bare essentials.

Milestones

1986 Endurance racing

Group C2 cars are the inspiration for the Ultima, built on a spaceframe chassis using Ford components, plus Renault rear suspension, transaxle and engine. It wins the kit car championship twice and spawns a Mk III with improved chassis and Rover or Chevrolet V8 power.

Ultima built its first vehicle back in 1986 for kit car racing.

1992 Ultima Sports is set up

in Hinckley, Leicestershire. It takes the existing Mk III Ultima and uses it to develop a street-legal version. Formula 1 designer Gordon Murray also uses the car as a base for developing the BMW V12 engine and transmission for the mighty McLaren F1 supercar.

The MK III Sports was used by McLaren as a testbed for the F1.

1993 The Mk IV Sports is

rebodied to form the Spyder, using the same chassis. It can be bought as either a kit or fully built.

UNDER THE SKIN

Featherweight

The foundation of the mid-engined Ultima is a separate tubular-steel perimeter chassis with two layers of 1.5-inch diameter, 16-gauge tubes. The massive roll bar helps to form a central survival cell, while there are deformable crumple zones in the front and rear. Ultima's own double wishbone suspension is used at both ends, with low-geared, rack-and-pinion steering, plus huge four-wheel AP Racing vented disc brakes.

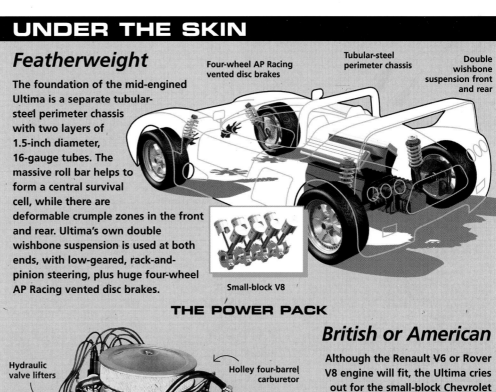

Four-wheel AP Racing vented disc brakes

Tubular-steel perimeter chassis

Double wishbone suspension front and rear

Small-block V8

THE POWER PACK

Hydraulic valve lifters

Holley four-barrel carburetor

Five main-bearing crankshaft

Cast-iron block and cylinder heads

British or American

Although the Renault V6 or Rover V8 engine will fit, the Ultima cries out for the small-block Chevrolet V8. Being mid-mounted, its bulk does not upset the weight distribution in the ultra-lightweight car. The age and tune depends on the customer, and so it can be mild or powerful, old or modern, with carburetors or fuel injection, and either cast-iron or alloy cylinder heads. Ultima recommends the HO version with 345 bhp and a single four-barrel Holley carburetor.

Open and closed

Ultimas are very unique cars; in fact, no two are likely to be the same. The final specification of each vehicle depends entirely on the requested options and budget of the new owner. The two main decisions are which body style—open or closed—and which engine. The Ultima can use just about any power you want, but the small-block Chevy V8 is the most powerful.

Both a Sports coupe and Spyder are offered by Ultima.

Ultima SPYDER

The style and shape of the Ultima has evolved over the years, inspired by the mighty Group C endurance racers that run at the 24 Hours of Le Mans. It also has the performance to back up its racy appearance and image.

Choice of engine

The Ultima is able to use a variety of engines. The ones usually specified are the Rover V8 in 3.5-, 3.9- or over 4.0-liter form, or a Renault V6 in up to 3.0-liter or 2.5-liter turbo form. The Renault has the advantage that it can be used with its own five-speed transaxle. For ultimate performance, however, a 350-cubic inch Chevy V8 can be installed.

Separate chassis

The main members in the separate tubular-steel chassis are composed of 1.5-inch steel tube. The chassis is calculated to be stiff enough to take the force of a 1000-bhp engine without distorting.

Front radiator

A large four-row radiator is mounted at the front, with its water pipes running around the outside of the chassis rails. Cooling is assisted by two thermostatically-controlled electric fans, and cut-outs in the front bodywork channel the air.

Porsche transaxle

To cope with the power and torque of the Chevrolet V8, a very strong transaxle is required. The best choice is the Porsche 911 unit. A special adapter plate is needed to mate the Chevy engine to the Porsche transaxle.

Tuned exhaust

The Chevrolet V8 needs a purpose-built exhaust system to fit in the Ultima. It consists of equal-length tubular headers connected to dual mufflers and pipes, inclined at an angle to fit under the engine cover.

Quick-release wing

Different rear wings can be fitted depending on use. For racing, a full-width wing will generate up to 1,000 lbs. of downforce at speed. Both types connect to a chassis-mounted pylon with quick-release pins, which means they can be detached in seconds.

Specifications

1998 Ultima Spyder

ENGINE

Type: Chevrolet V8

Construction: Cast-iron block and heads

Valve gear: Two valves per cylinder operated by a single camshaft with pushrods and rockers

Bore and stroke: 4.0 in. x 3.8 in.

Displacement: 5,733 cc

Compression ratio: 10.2:1

Induction system: Single Holley four-barrel carburetor

Maximum power: 345 bhp at 5,600 rpm

Maximum torque: 379 lb-ft at 3,600 rpm

TRANSMISSION

Porsche five-speed transaxle

BODY/CHASSIS

Separate tubular-steel chassis with fiberglass or Kevlar/carbon fiber bodywork

SPECIAL FEATURES

A racing-style fuel filler cap reflects the Ultima's roots in competition.

Fiberglass or composite bodywork is offered on both the coupe and Spyder.

RUNNING GEAR

Steering: Rack-and-pinion

Front suspension: Double wishbones with coil springs and telescopic shock absorbers

Rear suspension: Double wishbones with lower toe control link, coil springs and telescopic shock absorbers

Brakes: AP Racing vented discs, 12-in. dia. (front and rear)

Wheels: Alloy, 8 x 15 in. (front), 12 x 17 in. (rear)

Tires: 225/50 ZR15 (front), 315/35 ZR17 (rear)

DIMENSIONS

Length: 152.7 in. **Width:** 72.8 in.

Height: 42.1 in. **Wheelbase:** 110.0 in.

Track: 60.1 in. (front), 63.0 in. (rear)

Weight: 2,180 lbs.

Vector **W8-M12**

The best way of describing the exotic Vector is that it's America's answer to Lamborghini. It boasts phenomenal power output and has the performance to make it a contender for the title of the fastest car on earth.

"...American exotica."

"If you have ever wondered what a fighter pilot must feel like, slide into the Vector and you'll have a good idea. Everything is designed for ultra-high speeds. Its controls resemble those of a jet fighter and the overall ride is the same. As for the acceleration, it's American exotica that can compete with Italian supercars. The Vector offers unearthly performance and is a pleasure to drive—especially in the three digit mph range."

The Vector is by no means your everyday car. Inside it is more like a Space Shuttle than a conventional car.

Milestones

1977 Gerald A. Wiegert's
Vector W2 is presented in Los Angeles as "the fastest car in the world."

1990 After years
of preparation, the W8 is launched using a Donovan small-block Chevy®-designed engine.

Originally, Vectors were built with domestic drivelines.

1992 A WX3 model
has a new aerodynamic body, twin turbos and makes up to 1100 bhp.

1993 After a power struggle,
Megatech eventually emerges as the new owner and the company moves to Florida. Since they also own Lamborghini, future plans include building the car with the Diablo's V12. By using the underpowered Italian engine, the Vector will no longer be a full-blooded and extremely powerful U.S. supercar.

On looks, the Vector is a match for any Lamborghini or Ferrari.

1995 With a Diablo
492 bhp V12 engine and a much cheaper price tag, the new M12 model is marketed.

UNDER THE SKIN

Like an aircraft

Based in a part of California well known for its advanced aerospace industry, Vector took full advantage of its location. Under the super-lightweight composite bodywork there is an aircraft-inspired aluminum chassis which is both light and very strong. The Vector's running gear may be state of the art, but it is also practical. The front end boasts independent double-wishbone suspension, while the rear end consists of a well-located de Dion tube and coil/shock units.

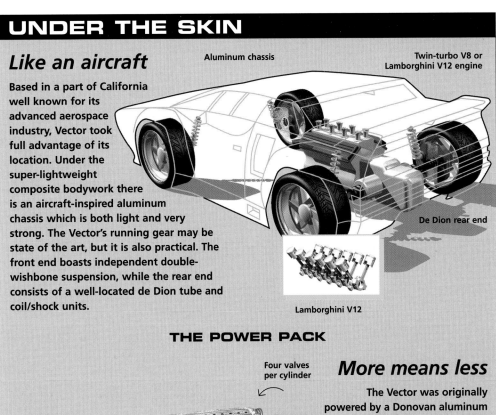

Aluminum chassis

Twin-turbo V8 or Lamborghini V12 engine

De Dion rear end

Lamborghini V12

THE POWER PACK

More means less

The Vector was originally powered by a Donovan aluminum engine based on Corvette's® 350 V8. It featured electronic fuel injection and twin turbochargers, with power ranging from 500 bhp to 1100 bhp. After a short production run using this engine, Vector Aeromotive was bought out and started using Lamborghini's Diablo 5.7-liter V12. Who would have thought that four extra cylinders from an Italian supercar company, would have cut the Vector's power output in half to 492 bhp?

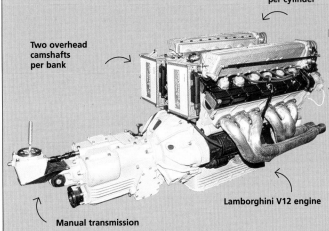

Four valves per cylinder

Two overhead camshafts per bank

Lamborghini V12 engine

Manual transmission

Vector M12

When Megatech acquired Vector Aeromotive, it restyled its body and gave it an Italian supercar engine. While the new body panels bring the car into the 1990s, it should have kept the 1,100-bhp Chevy-designed V8. In comparison, the new V12 only makes 492 bhp.

The M12 uses Lamborghini's bigger but less powerful V-12 engine.

Vector W8-M12

Originally marketed as an all-American supercar using a Chevy-designed engine and a Toronado® transmission, the Vector W8 pulled the rug out from under both Lamborghini and Ferrari.

Advanced bodywork

Years before other manufacturers began using sophisticated composites in cars, the Vector's bodywork contained Kevlar, fiberglass and carbon fiber.

Aircraft-influenced design

As well as using aerospace materials and construction methods, the Vector's styling also recalls aircraft practice.

Turbocharged Chevy V8

In a bid to make this an all-American supercar, the engine was derived from a Corvette V8 unit. To produce enough power to make this the fastest car in the world, Vector used twin intercooled Garrett H3 turbochargers.

Honeycomb chassis

The advanced chassis is a semi-monocoque structure. Like an aircraft frame, it is constructed from tubular steel and bonded aluminum honeycomb, and is extremely light and incredibly strong.

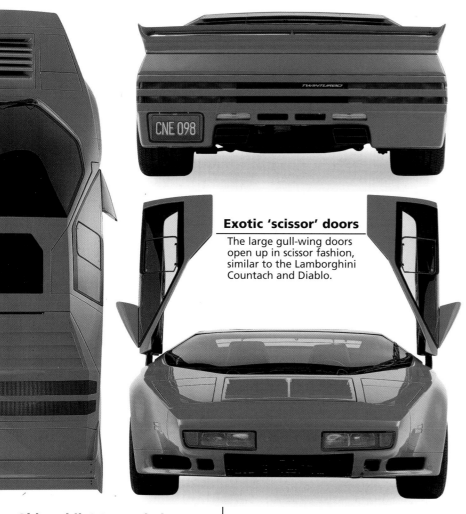

Exotic 'scissor' doors

The large gull-wing doors open up in scissor fashion, similar to the Lamborghini Countach and Diablo.

Oldsmobile® transmission

To transfer the immense power of the mid-mounted engine, Vector selected a suitably modified Toronado automatic transmission.

Powerful braking

With performance as breathtaking as the Vector's, brakes that can deal with speeds of up to 218 mph are required. The Vector has vented four-wheel discs measuring a massive 13 inches in diameter. Naturally, there is a sophisticated ABS system.

Specifications
1992 Vector W8

ENGINE

Type: V8

Construction: Cast-iron cylinder block and head

Valve gear: Two valves per cylinder operated by a single camshaft

Bore and stroke: 4.08 in. x 3.48 in.

Displacement: 5,973 cc

Compression ratio: 8.0:1

Induction system: Tuned port electronic fuel injection

Maximum power: 625 bhp at 5,700 rpm

Maximum torque: 630 lb-ft at 4,900 rpm

TRANSMISSION

Three-speed automatic

BODY/CHASSIS

Semi-monocoque honeycomb chassis with two-door coupe body in composite materials

SPECIAL FEATURES

Twin Garrett turbochargers can boost power up to 1100 bhp, a figure the Diablo engine could never match.

The radiator is mounted horizontally in the nose of the car, leaving little space for luggage up front.

RUNNING GEAR

Steering: Rack-and-pinion

Front suspension: Double wishbones with coil springs and shocks

Rear suspension: De Dion axle with longitudinal and transverse arms and coil spring/shock units

Brakes: Four-wheel discs

Wheels: Alloy, 16-in. dia.

Tires: 255/45 ZR16 front, 315/40 ZR16 rear

DIMENSIONS

Length: 172 in.   **Width:** 76 in.

Height: 42.5 in.   **Wheelbase:** 103 in.

Track: 63 in. (front), 65 in. (rear)

Weight: 3,572 lbs.

Venturi ATLANTIQUE

The Atlantique has carved a reputation as a highly accomplished mid-engined sports car capable of delivering the same performance and dynamic rewards as those produced by Ferrari, Lotus and Porsche.

"...delivers a mighty punch."

"Although the driving position is a little awkward, there's no argument about the performance. Following a small amount of lag, the engine rapidly builds boost and delivers a mighty punch. The archaic Renault transmission is notchy, but you soon forget about that in the delight of taking each challenging bend at a high rate of speed. The steering is very communicative, and the suspension offers handling that is comparable to the best."

The interior has cream-colored gauges and a tasteful wooden dashboard and console.

Milestones

1984 New company MVS presents the Ventury.

1986 Renamed the Venturi, France's newest sports car enters production.

1992 The Venturi-Larrousse Formula 1 racing team is formed, and the 400 GT racer arrives.

The Alpine A610 also used the Renault V6 engine.

1993 Venturi competes at Le Mans. Five of the seven entries complete the 24 Hour race.

1996 A Thai consortium takes over the company and presents the new Atlantique.

The 400GT boasted 408 bhp and carbon-fiber disc brakes.

1998 With twin turbochargers, the Atlantique 300 now develops an extra 25 bhp.

UNDER THE SKIN

Lotus-style construction

The Venturi's mid-engined layout is simple in design, and so are its underpinnings. The idea of a backbone steel chassis and fiberglass body was perfected by Lotus, and Venturi makes good use of this system. The suspension consists of double wishbones up front and two lower control arms at the rear, with coil springs and shock absorbers all around. Braking is courtesy of vented discs.

Double-wishbone front suspension

Separate backbone chassis

Four-wheel vented disc brakes

Mid-mounted V6

THE POWER PACK

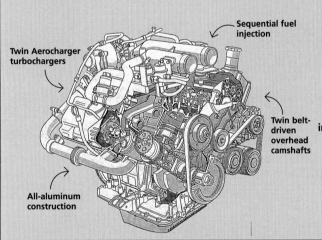

Sequential fuel injection

Twin Aerocharger turbochargers

Twin belt-driven overhead camshafts

All-aluminum construction

V6 twin turbo

The mid-mounted 3.0-liter engine owes little to the classic Renault/Peugeot V6 that powered previous Venturis. Constructed of aluminum, it features 24 valves, two overhead camshafts per bank of cylinders and sequential fuel injection. The secret of its impressive 302-bhp power output—which gives the Atlantique 300 its name—is twin Aerocharger intercooled turbochargers that use variable internal geometry to maintain near maximum power across a wide rpm range.

Venturi greats

Without question, the latest Atlantique 300 is the most satisfying Venturi to date. If you want a real Venturi delicacy, track down a rare convertible, but for a horsepower binge, there's the 400 GT. It has 408 bhp and carbon-fiber disc brakes.

The Atlantique has plenty of real-world power and finely developed dynamics.

Venturi ATLANTIQUE

The Atlantique name evokes images of Bugattis. The lightweight car has many qualities, including 302-bhp, balanced handling and a luxurious interior. But best of all, perhaps, is its exclusivity—only 250 cars are built each year.

Twin-turbo V6

The transversely mounted, centrally positioned engine is a specially developed 3.0-liter V6. Made of aluminum alloy, it manages to achieve its mighty 302-bhp power output with help from twin Aerocharger Aerodyne Dallas turbochargers.

Renault transmission

The five-speed manual transmission is based on Renault's well-known transaxle. This unit has been fitted to innumerable mid-engined sports cars largely because of its compact dimensions and an ability to withstand high power outputs.

Vented disc brakes

The large-diameter disc brakes are vented in the front and rear. Anti-lock braking is standard, and the whole system is dual-circuit and servo-assisted.

Composite plastic body

The Venturi has lightweight composite bodywork. This provides the benefits of quick development times, lower production tooling costs and more affordable materials. Much of the bodywork is strengthened, and the Venturi rates as one of the most rigid plastic-bodied cars ever made.

Complex suspension

The Venturi's underpinnings were originally designed by race car driver Jean Rondeau, but after his death, they were redeveloped by racers Mauro Bianchi and Jean-Pierre Beltoise. There are double wishbones up front and a sophisticated multi-link rear end consisting of an upper arm/tie bar and twin parallel lower arms located by an adjustable tie bar.

Aerodynamic shape

The Venturi's simple and understated shape was created by Gerard Godfroy, one of the founders of the company and an ex-employee of Peugeot. Extensive wind-tunnel testing has produced a very slippery car, which boasts a drag coefficient figure of just 0.31.

Specifications

1999 Venturi Atlantique 300

ENGINE

Type: V6

Construction: Aluminum block and heads

Valve gear: Four valves per cylinder operated by twin belt-driven overhead camshafts

Bore and stroke: 3.25 in. x 3.43 in.

Displacement: 2,946 cc

Compression ratio: 10.5:1

Induction system: Sequential fuel injection

Maximum power: 302 bhp at 5,500 rpm

Maximum torque: 298 lb-ft at 2,500 rpm

TRANSMISSION

Five-speed manual

BODY/CHASSIS

Separate backbone chassis with composite two-door coupe body

SPECIAL FEATURES

The Atlantique has four tailpipes; two on each side.

Engine-cooling vents are neatly incorporated into the styling.

RUNNING GEAR

Steering: Rack-and-pinion

Front suspension: Double wishbones with coil springs, telescopic shock absorbers and anti-roll bar

Rear suspension: Multi-link with coil springs and telescopic shock absorbers

Brakes: Vented discs (front and rear)

Wheels: Alloy, 17-in. dia.

Tires: 205/50 (front), 255/40 (rear)

DIMENSIONS

Length: 167.0 in.   **Width:** 72.5 in.

Height: 46.5 in.   **Wheelbase:** 98.5 in.

Track: 59.0 in. (front), 62.6 in (rear)

Weight: 2,750 lbs.